TALKS
for
LODGE and CHAPTER

Richard Sandbach
1996

©1996
Richard Sandbach

The rights of Richard Sandbach to be identified as author of this work has been asserted by him in accordance with the Copyright, Design and Patents Act, 1988.

First published in England in 1996
by Ian Allan Regalia Ltd
Coombelands House, Addlestone,
Surrey KT15 1HY
who are members of the Ian Allan Group.

ISBN 0 85318 216 7

Printed by Ian Allan Printing Ltd,
Coombelands House, Coombelands Lane, Addlestone, Surrey KT15 1HY

Contents

INTRODUCTION

Each paper in this book can be used as a talk on its own. I considered digesting the whole into one narrative but felt that it would be of more practical use in this form as a source which lodges could use when an alternative to a ceremony was required. Inevitably this has involved some duplication though that has been kept to a minimum and hopefully will not interfere with the enjoyment of those who may wish to read the work as a whole. For them, a word of explanation about the overall pattern is offered here.

Although each paper is separate and distinct an overall theme will be apparent, the desire to use the experience of the past and the practice of the present as a base for looking into the future with the object of assessing whether Freemasonry can reasonably expect to grow and flourish in the new century into which we are so rapidly moving and which will no doubt further advance the technological revolution which has been the dominant feature of the last quarter of the 20th century. It will only do so if it is seen as relevant to the needs of society in that century and this means it may have to adapt to some degree. That is a truism, as anyone who has had to do with the history of religions and social movements well known, but the immediate reaction of the average Freemason of today may be of the "Ils ne passeront" type. Such conservatism is understandable; the question is whether it will help or hinder the survival of Freemasonry. There is another question that must be answered in this connection: we cannot postulate that Freemasonry must survive and there are those who would prefer that it should not; we must therefore ask ourselves why it should do so?

The past is the parent of the present; and though it cannot control the future development of its offspring that development results largely from the wish to follow or to rebel. It became obvious that it was necessary to look back before we could look forward; there were three reasons for this: first, to see the extent to which change had taken place; second, to ascertain what were the true basic features whose sum produced the appeal of Freemasonry, because although the lessons of the past make it clear that a social phenomenon such as Freemasonry has to adapt to changing times as social needs and mores alter, if those changes challenge its basic tenets it will decay and die; and last, having decided what those basic factors are, what the aims of the Order have been, we must try to peer into the future and to assess how relevant they will continue to be.

This means looking back to origins before we can look forward to the future. We have to face the fact that the use of Freemasonry may have been exhausted so that it will have no place in that future, or that it may cease to be relevant to the needs of unborn generations. It would be sad if its usefulness in the future could be assured yet it decayed through lack of thought and a mindless elevation of the unessential into immutable law. Only by searching out the basic tenets about which we talk so glibly, and by resolutely acknowledging and promoting them can we establish whether Freemasonry can and should have a mission for the future and only with such knowledge can we look to that future.

Following on this line of thought, the first chapters delve into the past. My own views on our likely origins have been stated in a paper delivered to Quatuor Coronati Lodge in 1995 and a shortened version of that appears at the start of this work; other papers follow in that section covering related subjects. The developments of the 17th century have been fully covered so many times over that it seems pointless to enter into them again especially as much of the time was taken up by the quarrel between the two Grand Lodges, though it did see the development of the Third Degree and the coming of the Royal Arch. The lesson which was so painfully learned was the truth so often proved and so often ignored that disunited we cannot succeed. The reconciliation achieved in 1813 ended that chapter and marked a fresh beginning. There was little in this to affect the general theme with which we are here concerned, but the latter years of the Duke of Sussex's Grand Mastership saw a crisis of confidence and a challenge to the established order. It was an era which I see as formative in two respects: first because it saw the surge of rank-and-file insistence on their right to a part in the conduct of masonic affairs, which was bound to lead to a conflict with the authoritarian rule of the Duke of Sussex, however beneficial that rule might be, and second, as the proximate cause of the somewhat regressive and, I suggest, unimaginative regime enforced after the Duke's death by the Earl of Zetland in his long tenure of the Grand Master's throne (1844-1870).

Of the two main figures in that drama I had made a particular study: Bro the Reverend Dr George Oliver – "the sage and historian of Masonry" and probably the widest-read and most revered masonic author of the 19th century, and Bro Dr Robert Thomas Crucefix, the champion of the "Aged and Decayed Freemason", the swashbuckling challenger of the Duke of Sussex – or was he the idealist and reformer who rescued Freemasonry from torpor and decay? The two became firm friends; although they were so unlike in character they were united in their vision of Freemasonry. The brusque and sometimes overbearing procedures of the one contrast so vividly with the gentle scholarly attitude of the other that they make a fascinating picture and seen against the background of the towering, even domineering figure of Sussex anxious lest his work of unifying the Craft should be set at nought, it is no wonder that the scene was set for the drama which would have so marked an effect on the future of Freemasonry in England and Wales, not least in regard to the Knights Templar and the Ancient and Accepted Rite.

I have also tried to show something of the kind of background against which these developments were set, a background so different to that with which we are familiar that we have to make a serious effort to appreciate it, as we must if we are to understand the times and their constraints. For this reason too I have included the tour of Peterborough Cathedral, to show how, even in the later 19th century the Craft was allowed a public image and how late a development was the active discouragement of public interest in its affairs which was to prevail later and the effects of which are still felt today.

The Royal Arch deserves separate treatment but in looking to the future the same precepts apply as to the Craft and though some papers deal specifically with its future, in general those which try to look into that future and to suggest what may have to be done to adapt ourselves to survive in the next century, apply to both. Not everyone will accept the conclusions to which, however tentatively, I have come; but if they do me the honour of thinking constructively and so far as possible without prejudice about the issues raised my objective will have been achieved.

It goes without saying that I gladly give permission for the reading of any part of the book by way of a talk, though it would be appreciated if anyone doing so would make a donation to the Provincial Charity of the Province of Northamptonshire and Huntingdonshire, to whose Rulers I am happy to dedicate it (even without their prior permission).

Acknowledgements

Some of the papers in this book have appeared in *Ars Quatuor Coronatum* in whole or in part and the author is grateful to the Council of Quatour Correspondence Circle Ltd for permission to reproduce them.

PART ONE
ORIGINS

Any analysis or narrative should have a beginning, a middle and an end. For the student of the future of a social movement such as Freemasonry the beginning must be its origin, the middle must be its development and the end must be a projection into the future. At all stages of the journey the social and historical background will be important because without their setting figures and thoughts will be meaningless shadows, and any conclusions drawn may be falsely based.

The first evidence for the existence of a form of Freemasonry which we can recognise as such comes from the end of the 17th and start of the 18th centuries. Researchers differ over earlier happenings and their importance and the theory put forward in the first paper is only one of many. Its value for our purposes is that it provides a summary of the evidence and background; but the earnest seeker after knowledge might perhaps start his researches by referring to the full version mentioned in the headnote and to the authorities for other theories noted in it.

The second paper discusses the "landmarks" which are the undefined boundaries within which Freemasonry must remain if it is to remain "pure, ancient Freemasonry"; they are clearly of first importance in determining what can and what cannot be done. The last paper is concerned with the origins of Christian Orders of Freemasonry, the preservation of which was one of the prime reasons for the troubles which disturbed the last decade (1833-1843) of the Grand Mastership of the Duke of Sussex who, though an earnest Christian himself, had effectively achieved the removal of christian references from the Craft rituals. In the author's view those troubles and their consequences were of basic importance to masonic developments thereafter and still contain valuable lessons for us today.

1
Origins – the Craft

Any reader sufficiently interested in the subject can find the detailed paper of which this is a summary and references to other papers on the same subject, in Vol. 108 (1995) of Ars Quatuor Coronatorum, *the annually published report of the transactions of Quatuor Coronati Lodge 2076.*

We can start with one of the author's masonic rhymes:

> "Masonic origins have been the subject of disputes
> And fame awaits the Brother who all other claims refutes;
> But when for his achievement the brazen trumpets sound
> Their fanfare in his honour is likely to be drowned
> By laments from those researchers whose very, very best
> Occasion for disputing has at last been laid to rest."

That rhyme reflects the fact that there have been many theories about the origin of speculative Freemasonry, none of which have found universal approval; it is not improbable that there will be more and the theory to be advanced here is therefore only one of many. But even if the argument does not meet with approval it will serve a useful purpose in reviewing the evidence.

It will be as well at the start to state that the theory that is being put forward is that speculative Freemasonry has adopted the trappings of the operatives but did not directly descend from their lodges and had no independent existence before the last years of the 17th century. To support this it will be necessary to establish what we mean by speculative Freemasonry, to review the evidence (including the historical and social environment) and to consider something which has not always received the attention it deserves, the matter of motivation, for "the factor of secrecy [must have been] so powerful and pervasive as to have exerted an overwhelming influence down to the present day . . . There must have been compelling reasons for such secrecy at an early stage for it to have had so great an impact for so long, and they cannot be left out of consideration in seeking to uncover our origins." [*Bro Seal-Coon, commenting on a paper on our origins published in AQC in 1987.*]

We shall approach the problem on lines suggested by Bro Rudyard Kipling's well-known verse:

> "I keep six honest serving men
> (They taught me all I knew);
> Their names are What and Why and When
> And How and Where and Who."

First then, "WHAT?" This requires that we define the subject of the enquiry. In Bro Dyer's paper "Some Thoughts on the Origins of Speculative Masonry" given in Quatuor Coronati Lodge in 1982 [AQC 95] he defined Freemasonry as "that 'peculiar system of morality, veiled in allegory and illustrated by symbols' which has in the present day become an organisation, based on private lodges, under the control and government of The United Grand Lodge of England". This limits the scope of the enquiry sufficiently to require us to determine the point at which we find ourselves in touch with something we can recognise as a direct ancestor of our Freemasonry today and we may therefore adopt it.

Clearly the next serving man has to be WHEN: when did that something arise? Several theories have been advanced. A very popular one, supported by the late Bro Harry Carr, was the transitional theory which postulated a gradual takeover of operative lodges by non-operatives. Many doubts about this have been expressed. More recently an origin has been sought in inner circles of the medieval church, in the wish of men of goodwill to unite in troubled times, in architectural study circles or in the decay of the operative craft following the Reformation. All these have been the subject of recent papers but there does seem to have been confusion over what we mean by non-operative. For our purposes here let us stipulate that a non-operative is a man accepted as a member of a masonic organisation but who is not by trade or craft a Mason, while "speculative" means a Mason, whether operative or not, who acknowledges a "peculiar system of morality" as an essential ingredient of the Craft.

What then do we know about timing? First, we know that medieval operatives met in lodges. Then we have a record of a non-operative becoming a Mason – "being made a Mason" in the terms they used – in 1646. Fortunately he is a man about whom a great deal is known and so we come to the next serving man, WHO. Elias Ashmole was an officer in the royalist army who had been captured at Worcester and in October 1646 he was on parole in Cheshire. The "making" took place in Warrington, the site of a major bridge across the river Mersey. The record comes from his diary but in quoting it I am substituting the word "Master" for the abbreviation "Mr". The Oxford English Dictionary indicates that this was what the abbreviation stood for in that time and the matter, as we shall see, may be important. Here then is the entry: "I was made a Free Mason at Warrington in Lancashire, with Coll: [that is, Colonel] Henry Mainwaring of Karincham in Cheshire. The names of those that were then of the Lodge. Master Rich [that is Richard] Penket Warden, Master James Collier, Master Rich Sankey, Henry Littler, John Ellam, Rich Ellam & Hugh Brewer."

Ashmole would later become an important man, a member of the Royal Society and founder of the Ashmolean Museum among other achievements. Colonel Mainwaring, who was related to him by marriage, had been very active in the parliamentary cause but may by this time have become disenchanted by it. There are differing theories about the identity of the others but without going into detail here, it seems clear that they were a social and probably political mix; for instance, the last four named have not been given the title of "Master" and at least one may have been an operative Mason. But clearly not only was some sort of ceremony involved which must have had an operative origin, but by this time the phrase "made a Free Mason" was probably in common use, facts which suggest that this was already an established procedure.

9

It is important to realise Ashmole's situation at the time. He was about to ride south to London. The country he would have to traverse was in the hands of the parliamentary forces, who were somewhat discontented, not having been paid. In London the Parliament was considering and indeed passing radical laws about religion, making a failure to support some doctrines a capital matter attracting the death penalty. The king was a captive of the Scottish army at Newcastle-on-Tyne. The country, as events of the next years would show, was one step away from anarchy.

Now we advance 40 years to 1686, 26 years after the Restoration of Charles II and two years before the abdication of James II, when an antiquarian, Dr Robert Plot, published a book called *The Natural History of Staffordshire*. In it he made a number of statements about Freemasonry. The most important for our purposes now are, first, that he indicated that the practice of making Masons was widespread, not only in Staffordshire but all over England, and second, that the persons so made included what he called "persons of the most eminent quality". He also gave a partial description of the ceremony of "making" and this brings us to the next serving man, HOW, because if we know what anyone made a Mason might expect to learn in the process it may throw light on the vital question of WHY such men wished to be "made" which we shall have to consider later.

Plot asserts that a meeting attended by what he calls "five or six of the Antients of the Order" was held and certain signs were communicated to the candidate [and now I quote] "whereby they are known to each other all over the nation, by which they have maintenance whither ever they travel". He also mentions in scathing terms a volume containing the ancient history of Freemasonry which was brought to the notice of the candidate. This would suggest that an Initiate, as we would call him today, would learn two things, the recognition secrets and the contents of the volume.

We know quite a lot about this volume and a number of such documents have survived, generically known as "Ancient Charges" or "Old Charges". They can be dated over a period from the early 16th century (which means there were earlier ones) to the late 17th century and even into the 18th. In his 1982 paper Bro Dyer showed that over a period they changed their form and he concluded that whereas the earliest were prepared for use in an operative lodge, there was a gradual development to adapt the contents to serve "a group or movement . . . moral in object . . . [and which] clearly had . . . some religious significance". We may reasonably infer that admission of non-operatives as Masons had already begun by the middle of the 16th century and had continued well into the middle of the 17th. This does not necessarily mean that lodges were changing their membership from operative to non-operative though the growth of what Dyer called "new articles" in the later copies made it possible for him to assert that by the mid-17th century (and here I quote) "here is a Masonry that is recognisable as the forerunner of a more modern Craft": to which we may add, "Yes, but a forerunner, not necessarily an ancestor". However, these "new articles" are exactly the sort of tightening up of earlier exhortations about behaviour which one would expect if it was felt that entry into the fraternity should be more strictly controlled; but, with one possible exception which we shall come to, there is no firm evidence yet of regular meetings of masonic lodges of any type; nor have we evidence yet of any "system of morality".

So far we have concentrated on the English picture, but we know that masonic lodges existed elsewhere and the claims of Scotland in particular have been pressed as an origin of Freemasonry, so we must now consider the next serving man, WHERE?

In the 17th century most of the population of England lived around London, then the biggest city in Western Europe, and most of the remainder was in the south-west. The Midlands and North were relatively lightly peopled. It is therefore in London that we would expect to find evidence of the existence of any organised non-operative Freemasonry and there is in fact presumptive evidence that by the latter half of the century there was an inner circle of the London Company of Masons known as "the Acception" which was admitting non-operatives as Freemasons. Ashmole attended the admission of a number of them on 10th March 1682, four years before the publication of Plot's book, and we should note that he seems to have been entitled to do so by reason of his "making" more than 30 years before.

In Scotland, where the Schaw statutes of 1598 and 1599 required lodges to keep records of meetings, these provide evidence of frequent lodge meetings in the 17th century. Dr Stevenson, reader in Scottish History at the University of Aberdeen, who is not a Freemason but has written about the history of the Scottish Craft, lists a number of cases where non-operatives were admitted into Scottish lodges in this period; but only in a few of these do the non-operatives seem to have been regular attenders or to have remained members for long. It is difficult to accept that such admissions arose from any cause other than the patronage which was deeply engrained in the Scottish social system and perhaps curiosity about a "mason word". There seems to be no evidence that anything like speculative Freemasonry was involved or that Scottish practice spread south to England. In the absence of evidence to the contrary we may fairly presume that speculative Freemasonry in England developed there as an indigenous social phenomenon.

We have seen that it seems reasonably certain that in England non-operatives were being "made" from at least the middle of the 17th century and probably for a considerable time before that; but we still have to investigate when men so "made" began to meet together in lodges and evolve the "system of morality" which grew to become the English speculative Freemasonry of today.

It is important to remember that speculative Freemasonry as we know it is a social phenomenon and could therefore only have developed in harmony with its environment, as indeed it must continue to do if it is to survive. So we turn again to another serving man, WHEN?

Consider the historical background. By 1530 the Reformation had been precariously established. A reversion to catholicism followed under Mary (1553-1558) after which protestantism returned under Elizabeth I and an attempted Spanish invasion was dramatically defeated in 1588 leaving the country free to develop its genius. When James VI of Scotland succeeded to the English throne in 1603 he came from a country in which a presbyterian system of christian worship had been established. His successor, Charles I, was an autocrat whose policy on religion was suspect for both episcopalians and presbyterians. Civil war broke out in 1642; the king was defeated in 1646, the year of Ashmole's "making", and executed in 1649. England came under parliamentary rule, at first that of religious bigots but eventually under the effective control of Cromwell. Scotland briefly acknowledged Charles II. In 1660 Charles was restored to both thrones. London launched itself into an era of scientific, academic and social exuberance. In 1662 the Royal Society received its first royal charter; interestingly, discussion of religion and politics was not allowed at its meetings. In 1665 the great plague ravaged the country. In the following year the great fire of London destroyed the centre of the capital and a revival of operative masonry followed. Charles died in 1685 and was succeeded by his brother, James VII & II, who was suspected of intending to return the realm to Roman catholicism and of a wish to restore absolutism. The West, the most densely populated part of the kingdom outside the London area, rose in rebellion and was bloodily defeated. In 1688 James was forced from the throne into exile where he and his family would be an ever-present menace for the next half-century until the battle of Culloden in 1746. It is against this background of challenge, change, despotism, bigotry and violence in a country which within the short space of a century had known the excitement of the reign of the first Elizabeth, a vicious civil war, the execution of one king and the expulsion of another, that our investigations are taking place and we have to reconcile the "makings" of the earlier 17th century with the emergence of non-operative lodges towards its end.

In the late 17th century there was great interest in every sort of knowledge and particular interest in philosophical and scientific matters. A mental fever of curiosity enveloped England as the spiritual inheritors of the Renaissance eagerly resumed the quest for learning which the quarrels of the disastrous first half of that century had so drastically curtailed; the Age of Reason followed when the society of coffee house and club held sway. Argument of every description flourished. When "persons of the most eminent quality" who had been "made" found themselves in company together it would be natural to discuss Freemasonry and the morality and history taught in the Ancient Charges.

So now we come to our last serving man, WHY, with two questions: Why did the early non-operatives such as Ashmole seek to become Masons? and Why did such men turn their masonic involvement into the system of morality we know today?

It will be simpler to deal with this latter question first. If what has already been suggested is accepted, the answer to why English speculative Freemasonry could have grown at the end of the 17th century from early "makings" is clear. The inquisitive and social spirit of the age would ensure that men would gather together and discuss philosophical and scientific questions. When two or more found that they had masonic knowledge in common, it would be natural to arrange to meet privately to discuss Freemasonry; and at such meetings, after the inevitable feast, what was there to discuss other than what they had learned when they were "made" and perhaps their use of the recognition signs? The mythical history would of course get embellished as providing the respectability of antiquity; and the moral code would be embroidered and extended by reference to biblical exhortations because the Bible was regarded as the ultimate and definitive authority in moral matters. With the example of the London Company before the inhabitants of the capital the possibility of organisation into coherent groups would be an obvious choice. It requires no great imaginative leap to see in this the start of such a movement as that which has developed into the English speculative Freemasonry of today and some words of Bro Dyer's may support this suggestion; he wrote "Bro Carr claims that I have based my paper on the idea that there were but two phases in our masonic history: nothing is further from the truth – the paper is concerned to show that operative masonry had no part at all in the origins of the movement which has become the English Freemasonry of today other than the copying of some of its procedures and tools in allegory."

We still have to find some reason why non-operatives became Freemasons in the first place and that reason must be strong enough to explain why their interest was sustained until the public emergence of some embrionic form of speculative Freemasonry. This implies something more than idle curiosity, a wish to acquire purported esoteric knowledge, a hankering after insubstantial moral teaching or an interest in a mythical history of doubtful accuracy. The "makings" continued over a considerable time: had there been either no valid reasons for their continuing popularity or any disappointment in what was achieved they would have ceased.

So why did those early non-operatives and their successors, many of them persons of importance, seek admission to groups initially established for and peopled by men with whom they seem to have had so little in common? We now have to draw conclusions from the evidence and in doing so we must be analytical and avoid the trap of trying to make the evidence fit preconceived ideas. In fact, it is time to put my conclusions forward for your consideration.

First then we can note that there is a clear link between the "makings" of the earlier years and the later form which was developing into speculative Freemasonry at the end of the century, insofar as the speculative Freemasons who practiced their craft in the 18th century made symbolic use of masonic material in their rituals and had some knowledge of the ways of the operatives. This gives rise to a presumption that the non-operatives made in the earlier period had something to do with the events of the later part, especially as we have Plot's evidence about the growth of masonic membership and the fact of Ashmole's attendance at a meeting in London in 1682. He, and others whom we know to have been "made" in that earlier period, were men of intelligence and unlikely to have been attracted by the possibility of acquiring mystical knowledge. Besides, Plot clearly shows that a contempt for the Ancient Charges was found among serious students. That leaves the means of recognition as the only other knowledge acquired at the ceremony; so we have to ask why men would wish to acquire such knowledge and that involves asking what practical use it would be to them. There are two points to note here; first there are the dangers of travel and the turmoil of the times; and second, the fact that Ashmole was "made" immediately before starting on what might be a hazardous journey – (he may even have waited to start until he had been "made"?) That travel was indeed hazardous we may see from a quotation from *Travel in England* by Thomas Burke. Writing of Stuart times he says "The dangers of travel were so much recognised that any man going on a journey could, on a request to the vicar of his parish, have prayers offered for his safety." – and that was in time of peace.

So it seems logical to say that there must have been a link between these early "makings" and what happened in the latter part of the century for two reasons: first, because at the end of the century there would be a number of men in London, where the bulk of the population was, who had been "made" and would get to know each other, sometimes perhaps through the meetings of the London Acception; and second because of the atmosphere of clubs and coffee-houses that prevailed there. In the secrecy enjoined upon them at their "making" they could share their experiences and the knowledge of masonic tradition they had then imbibed; and it can surely not be thought of as doing too much violence to academic asceticism to suggest that they might even get some enjoyment out of mystifying those outside the charmed circle. Nor would it be strange that with such a background as that of the Acception they should use the term "lodge" for their clubs.

Is there anything in the evidence which conflicts with this theory? I suggest there is not. In 1646 Ashmole's circumstances were such that any assurance of safety for his journey would be welcome. Plot's evidence suggests that the fact that non-operatives were being "made" masons was at best an open secret and that there had been many "makings", including men of note. As to other theories, let me pose two questions: would members of a society which was trying to keep its existence secret have recruited across social and political boundaries in this way? and if there was a cause to support, what was it and why does Ashmole not refer to it or do anything to foster it? The fact that in 1698 a pamphlet appeared in London warning the public against "those called Freed-Masons" who met "in secret places and with secret signs" seems to confirm rather than contradict the theory and once again we can notice the emphasis on secret signs.

As to ideas more recently put forward, that our origins are to be found in the coming together in troubled and distressing times of men of goodwill who wished to bring religious and political strife to an end, evidence to support it is lacking and Plot's remarks, insofar as they are acceptable, seem to point us in an opposite direction. Experience suggests that if such a movement does not succeed it will falter and die, particularly if it is secretive, and if any such movement did succeed it is unlikely that it could go unnoticed in a century of such turbulence and with extensive spy systems being operated by successive governments; nor does such a theory explain why the system it postulates should change its nature and develop into speculative Freemasonry as we now know it.

It is suggested therefore that on the basis of the factual evidence we can reasonably adopt as a working hypothesis the theory that the emergence of truly speculative Freemasonry as already defined began during the last decade of the 17th century and the first of the 18th in the prevalent atmosphere of clubs and coffee-houses among men who, probably for practical reasons of personal safety, had been "made" masons in earlier, chaotic times.

So to a conclusion. The result of my heretical speculations can be very simply stated. In 17th century England, where political and religious factors as well as outright villainy could spell danger for a stranger in an unknown place, anything which guaranteed a safe lodging and freedom from betrayal to enemies or rogues would be a great boon. That was precisely what the operative Masons could offer to those possessing the masonic recognition secrets, and it would be a powerful reason for men to wish to be "made" when once the operatives began to accept non-operatives as candidates. Later, after the defeat of James VII and II at the battle of the Boyne in 1690 and as the Age of Reason dawned and the country settled down, social contacts in the main areas of population, and particularly in London, would lead to discussion among non-operatives so "made"; and with the example of the "Acception" at Masons Hall before them on which they could build, a wish to have the independence of one's own lodge, with one's own friends, and perhaps even to boast of secret knowledge, would be a natural result. In the climate of the times the emergence of speculative Freemasonry as defined would be an almost inevitable consequence.

Such a theory does not necessarily run counter to the work of established masonic scholars who in greater or lesser degree seek to ascribe a religious origin to the masonic movement (to use a hopefully neutral word) as it was in the late 16th century, for such views only relate to the survival of Masonry in the 15th and 16th centuries so that it still existed recognisably in the 17th. If established, such activity might explain why the lodges in which non-operatives would later be "made" survived. Nor does it run counter to Bro Dyer's views if I have correctly interpreted them, for in the paragraph of his paper headed "CONCLUSION" he stated his tentative view that the movement which gave rise to speculative Masonry was a deliberate creation which arose in the first 20 years or so of the reign of the first Elizabeth and that changes of a radical nature which occurred probably in the 1660s brought at least some part of speculative Masonry into a form recognisable as an early predecessor of the present English Craft. This paper seeks answers to two supplementary questions: first why the growth of "making" or accepting as Masons men of good social status should have accelerated in the early part of the 17th century (largely it would seem before the Restoration of Charles II in 1660); and second why such men should later have grouped themselves together to form lodges which had such permanence that some of them still exist today. The answer proposed necessarily implies that the transition theory is unlikely to be soundly based, that Freemasonry as defined can only have come into existence in the late 17th century at the earliest and that its sole connection with the ancient craft of Masonry is that it bases its teaching and its symbolism on what its early progenitors had learned and developed from their association with a craft in which neither they nor those who introduced them as members had any intention that they should serve apprenticeships or try to earn a living as operative Masons – a sort of apostolic rather than hereditary succession.

This theory seems to the author of this paper not only to be supported by the evidence but – and herein lies the greatest heresy – more plausible than either the transitional, the conspiracy or the do-good theories, if only because it is more consonant with human nature and the casual, rather than plotted, development which we associate with the English temperament in general. It will of course be opposed by those who seek a grander origin; but such a search has its own inbuilt bias and in research bias is the enemy of truth. All I claim is that, given the known facts, the suggestion is consistent with the evidence, with the social environment, with human nature, and with a truth which we are often too proud to acknowledge – that in the world of social evolution to which the problem of our origins rightly belongs, events are more often shaped by circumstances than by polices.

There is one final point to make. These suggestions may be seen by some as attacking the antiquity of Freemasonry. In truth, they preserve it, showing that our new building rests on old and secure foundations of which we can be as proud as we can of the system we have erected on them.

2
"Do not move the Ancient Landmarks"?

The importance of considering the "Ancient Landmarks" in any assessment of a future for freemasonry is their immovability. As is constantly stressed in these papers, if Freemasonry is to survive it must remain relevant to the society in which it is set though it may be selective as to which of the habits of that society it supports. While certain basic standards may be regarded as essential, many customs and habits will change with the years. It would be wrong to assume that Freemasonry has not adapted to this and fatal to assume that it never should. If the landmarks are too widely drawn the result will be to prevent the possibility of change. Where then should the lines be drawn?

The dilemma about the ancient landmarks of Freemasonry can be expressed in terms of a verse I wrote some time ago:

> "Do not move the ancient landmarks":
> Down the years the voices ring.
> But – what are the ancient landmarks?
> Well, that's quite another thing.

Of necessity, what I have to say will be a personal view but I hope it will give you something to think about; and let me reassure any doubters that masonic research does not endanger your health.

There are two major points to clarify before we can discuss the importance or even existence of masonic landmarks. The first is to try to decide what a landmark is and the second to consider the relevance of landmarks. It will be necessary to go into detail about matters with which many of you may already be familiar but as a knowledge of them is essential if we are to understand the problem, you will I hope pardon me if I recall them to your notice once again.

Taking the first point, what is a landmark? No-one seems to have produced a definitive definition and that of itself suggests that there is scope for disagreement, so perhaps instead of trying to find a definition we should spend some time thinking about what is the purpose of these mysterious items which are so revered by Freemasons, and we start with the Book of Constitutions, which in this case certainly does not live up to the role in which it is recommended to the newly installed Master – the solver of all problems.

Rule 125 is quite clear about one thing however, namely that a belief in TGAOTU is an essential landmark. It does this in a roundabout way by stating the qualifications a man must possess before he can be admitted as a visitor to a Private Lodge held under the jurisdiction of The United Grand Lodge of England; one of those qualifications is that he has been initiated in a Lodge belonging to (an odd phrase, that) belonging to a Grand Lodge professing a belief in TGAOTU and "shall acknowledge that [such a] belief is an essential Landmark of the Order". So here we have an acknowledgement in the somewhat oblique way of the existence of landmarks in general (for the rule refers to "an essential Landmark" not to "the essential Landmark"), and a statement of one.

Then we have two other references to landmarks, each imposing responsibility on someone for preserving the landmarks but neither shedding any light on the question of what is a landmark or giving any guidance on how to recognise one. These two references are in rule 55 (which gives an absolute power to The Grand Master to refuse permission for anything to be discussed at a Quarterly Communication of the Grand Lodge if it "contains anything contrary to the antient Landmarks of the Order") and in rule 111 (which requires that before he can be installed a Master Elect "shall solemnly pledge himself to observe the Landmarks of the Order, to observe the antient usages and established customs, and strictly enforce them within its own Lodge"). You will have noticed two things about this: first, that the reference here is to a landmark, which raises the question of whether there are landmarks other than the "antient" ones, so let me make it clear that in this paper "landmark" means an "antient" landmark; second that a landmark is distinguished here from "antient usages and established customs", an important matter since it makes it clear that antiquity alone cannot qualify a particular item as a landmark. This second point challenges a number of things we might (or someone else might, because this can be a very subjective exercise) claim to be landmarks. Finally in this context we should note that the Grand Lodge itself is bound by these mysterious things, for rule 4, which states that the supreme superintending authority in the Order is vested in the Grand Lodge and that it and it alone can enact laws and regulations for the government of the Craft, requires that, in exercising those powers, it must always "take care that the antient Landmarks of the Order be preserved".

So how far has this preliminary examination of the problem taken us? I suggest that it has shown that nothing can be an antient landmark unless it is so basic to Freemasonry that it must have been in existence at the beginning of speculative Freemasonry. Some might wish to take it further and claim that only something which can be shown to have existed in operative Masonry can be any kind of landmark, but there are even more problems here for we now come up against the question of whether there is in fact a direct link between speculative Freemasonry and the operative Masonry of medieval times and that takes us into very deep water. Answers vary, because it all depends on what we mean by Freemasonry. Dr Oliver considered it to be the developed form of the rules of conduct laid down at the Creation, which in his day was considered to have occurred in 4000 BC, or if you were very up-to-date, in 4004 BC. Upholders of what is known as the transitional theory, popularised by the late Bro Harry Carr, consider that speculative Freemasonry developed within the operative lodges; unreliable tradition places the origin of these in Anglo-Saxon times and according to legend they could be traced back to King Solomon's time. These theories would effectively rule out most candidates as landmarks and so we have to consider more precisely what we mean by speculative Freemasonry in this context. I am going to be quite arbitrary about this and state that there seems to me to be no point in considering anything earlier than the medieval operatives lodges as providing our speculative origin; on this basis we cannot date our beginnings back earlier than the Plantagenet kings. If anyone wants to dispute that I am quite willing to argue the point if he will state his case, but as this talk must remain within reasonable limits I state that assumption and move on, only remarking that those who press the case for earlier origins are usually equally pressing about the need to preserve the landmarks, not seeing that the further back in time you go the fewer the landmarks you can prove to have existed.

So we start with the Middle Ages. There was a great deal of building in England then and masons were in great demand. The buildings were usually of considerable size and cost a great deal of money, not least in many cases for transport and materials. They would generally be ecclesiastical, varying from small parish churches to cathedrals with monastic buildings, castles, or such places as guild halls, and the work would often take a considerable time to complete. During that time the masons would need accommodation in which they could keep their tools, work on the stone, shelter, meet for discussion and food, even perhaps sleep. This need was satisfied by the erection of a shed or small building, called the masons' lodge and the term of course still persists today and could perhaps be some sort of landmark.

Now the masons were craftsmen and their craft had to be learned. The learning took place on site, as it were, and this would give rise to a distinction between the trained and untrained man. A ceremony was apparently devised to mark the transition from apprentice to fellow craft; I am not stating categorically that those were the terms used in early days, though they definitely appear later. There may also have been a ceremony when a man, probably a youth, was bound to his master as an apprentice; ceremonials have long been used to mark important events in life and these are generically referred to as "rites of passage". Apart from those relating to death, their object is usually twofold: to impress on the individual the importance and nature of the obligations he or she is undertaking, and to give public notice of the relationship. In the case of masons, the duties with which members of the fraternity expected their colleagues to comply were apparently expressed in writing, and by the time of Queen Elizabeth the First these written statements seem to have achieved a formal status; they contained a history of the craft of masonry and rules of conduct for masons. These are the documents we now call the Old Charges or Ancient Charges.

The history given in these Charges is considered by scholars to be mythical; it purports to trace organised Masonry in England back to King Athelstan's time and even earlier. Its importance is that it shows the pride the masons took in their craft and their insistence on its respectability and independence. The rules of conduct are more important for the purpose of our enquiry than the mythical history.

A considerable number of these documents have survived, dating over a period from the 15th to the 17th centuries. Bro Colin Dyer, in a paper delivered in Quatuor Coronati Lodge in 1980, showed that over that period they changed considerably and that in the later years the rules became more stringent. The earlier versions of the rules contained a variety of clauses the general import of which was that masons should live good lives, do their jobs well and be faithful to their fellows. Later versions insisted on such things as proceedings at the acceptance (to use one of the terms then current), the acceptance of a man as a Mason, the qualifications for that acceptance, and the government of the lodge. One such rule may interest you; it required a Mason "to receive and cherish Fellowes when they come over the countreyes" and "sett them work, if they will" – which might create some difficulty today.

So, have we found something that we can regard as speculative Freemasonry? There may be likenesses but they are embryonic; and, well, there is a problem. We know that by the middle of the 17th century non-masons were being accepted as Masons and there are good reasons for thinking that this may have been done ceremonially in lodges and, originally at least, by operatives, such as those whom Dr Plot, an antiquary who wrote in 1686, referred to as "the Ancients of the Order", a phrase which in these days, like later references to "The Asylum for Aged and Decayed Freemasons" may bring a wry smile to the lips of the more elderly among us. But we have no evidence that such men became members of the lodge or that the lodges met at regular intervals or that there was a standard procedure other than the possession at the ceremony of a version of the Old Charges and the communication of the recognition secrets. In fact the evidence is all the other way, with one possible exception which we must now consider.

In London there had since the 15th century been a Guild of Masons, meeting at Masons' Hall and they had a mysterious body known as the Acception which met when required, though apparently not with any regularity. By the latter part of the 17th century it was making masons of non-operatives. But we do not certainly know when or why this began nor is there evidence of anything we would recognise as regular meetings, using "regular" in the sense of periodic. But men who had been accepted as Masons in other parts of the country were allowed to attend these ceremonies and so we appear to have confirmation of earlier evidence that there were indeed recognition signs in use. Have we something here we can accept as speculative Freemasonry? Possibly, though the author's view, for reasons which it would take too long to explain now, is that we have not yet reached that stage. However, if for the purpose of argument we can accept it in that sense, it is the earliest time when we have evidence of a consistent sequence of non-operative masonic meetings which we can, by stretching our imaginations, consider as such, and the implication would be that our landmarks must have been in existence by about the middle of the 17th century.

What would that mean in practice? Assuming – and it is in every sense an assumption – that the meetings of the Acception took a similar form to that described by Dr Plot it appears to suggest that it limits us to considering only three things, the basic moral rules, the essentials for what we would now call Initiation, and the nature and sanctity of the recognition signs. Of the signs we have no sure knowledge, but if you suspect, as I do, that the lodges which were formed in the closing years of the 17th and early years of the 18th centuries were often founded by men who had been accepted as Masons in the earlier part of the 17th century in lodges which often had some trace of operative background, it is not unreasonable to suppose that the recognition secrets, at least the grip, and perhaps a word or words were used by the operatives. It is also possible that items from Scottish Freemasonry may later have been incorporated but if you accept my thesis so far, it will not matter whether England or England and Scotland provided the raw material; the governing factor would be inclusion at the time when speculative Freemasonry made its appearance.

We can also assume that certain items of ceremony would survive. But unless we accept that in fact the speculative Freemasonry we know, the system of morality founded on brotherly love, relief and truth, only came into existence later, in the closing years of the 17th century at the earliest, we have to conclude that only three, or at the most four, items qualify: a belief in God, the recognition secrets, the requirement of a formal Initiation, and perhaps some of the moral content of the Old Charges. However, if we accept that speculative Freemasonry as an organised system did not exist until shortly before the founding of the Premier Grand Lodge in 1717, as I have argued elsewhere, a rather different picture is presented and to that we now turn.

If speculative Freemasonry is a system built on ancient foundations, but in itself a new structure originating shortly before 1717, then the antient landmarks are to be found in the context of that structure. We have therefore to consider what it was that our predecessors were building into it. For the purpose of this part of the argument I am taking as fact something to which I have already referred to briefly but which not everyone involved in masonic research is ready yet to accept, namely that the men who, whether they realised exactly what they were doing or not, first began to practise what has become speculative Freemasonry, had been initiated in ceremonies which were essentially based on the ceremonial used by the operative masons. In that case they would consider themselves as practising what they had been taught, which, in addition to the recognition secrets and the obligation not to disclose them to non-masons, would basically be the mythical history of the Craft and the rudimentary rules of conduct in the Old Charges. As we have seen they contained a detailed legend purporting to show how the Craft had been derived from ancient days and often from biblical times; they varied somewhat in this – some went back to the Tower of Babel and the Flood, and most seem to have included references to Euclid and Pythagoras as skilled in the art. They detailed how the skills involved in building King Solomon's Temple had been brought to England and nurtured here by the patronage of monarchs. We have also noted that they contained moral injunctions which related to such things as behaviour to employers, superiors and fellow workmen and generally urged the individual to be honest and worthy. These latter were the rules which showed pronounced development over the 16th and 17th centuries, particularly in respect of the qualifications for membership and the government of the lodge. There was no standard version though the general content was substantially the same: the antiquity and importance of the craft, its structure, and a greater or lesser degree of what we might call moral musing. But the lack of uniformity means in my view that, as I have said, they can hardly qualify as a landmark.

Now the last years of the 17th century saw the growth of great interest in all kinds of abstract thought and such matters as astrology and alchemy, but particularly in philosophy, which for this purpose we may think of as the business of asking questions about existence in general and that of the human race in particular, as well as about the universe in which that existence is set. Much of the thought and theory was centred on London, then the largest city in Europe and a hot-bed of discussion and argument. Men of outstanding intellect and ability abounded: Newton, Wren and Pepys to name but three; and around them was a throng of men anxious for knowledge and alert to question. The coffee houses where they all met were typical of the social life of the city and many clubs were formed, some of which, such as the Royal Society, lasted while others were ephemeral. The troubled years of the earlier part of the century with its civil war and religious quarrels, and the social upheavals which came in their wake had halted the ebullience and excitement of the Elizabethan period and as it were bottled up the enthusiasm and outpouring of genius which had distinguished the intellectual life of that era. With the return of peace the pent in powers were released and London was in a ferment which neither the plague nor the great fire could suppress. In this atmosphere intelligent men who had in more unsettled times sought admission to the secrets of the operative Masons, for whatever reason, would be meeting one another, they had been bound to secrecy, so meetings arranged between them might often be private in order that they might discuss their masonic experiences. In the background was the London Company of Masons, with its mysterious "Acception" into which non-operatives were admitted from time to time. It seems to me that it would be inevitable that such men would arrange to meet in groups and would form clubs; it would be likely that they would call these groups by the traditional name of lodges. In these lodges they could discuss what they had learned from the operatives and decide what were the essentials for holding a lodge, what should be the qualifications for admitting others to their circle and what those admitted should be taught; as the number of lodges increased they may also have thought about what the criteria were by which one group would recognise another as what we now call regular, something which may have been a factor in the formation of the Premier Grand Lodge in 1717. Now all this is supposition on my part but I suggest to you that something of this sort most probably happened.

If against this background clubs were formed among those who found themselves to be fellow-masons some things would be virtually certain to follow. The obligation of secrecy about the signs affected them all and they seem to have taken it seriously – and they may indeed have enjoyed putting on an air of mystery and superiority. As these meetings and clubs developed into lodges, what would be the characteristics the members would adopt? It is unlikely that there would be much co-ordination between them at that early stage, though there were signs in the later Old Charges of an attempt to impose some sort of discipline. But there would certainly be a wish to consolidate their claims to a venerable antiquity and descent by stressing their links with the operative Craft, and this meant links with building and with the working tools of the building trade, which could be used to emphasise the high moral purpose of the members, and some kind of acceptance of the Old Charges. Similarly, because they would wish to bind new entrants to the secrecy which governed them, the Bible would have to be exhibited and open in Lodge. A belief in God was enjoined by the Old Charges; that, of course, was in the context of Christianity but any limitation to a particular religious belief must have ceased to be a landmark, if it ever was one, or even an ancient usage a century later when under the eagle eye and forceful direction of the Duke of Sussex all christian references were supposed to be removed from the ritual, an event which was indeed challenged at the time as the removal of a landmark.

Then there was the question of the government of the lodge. There seems to have been some variation in this; for instance, when Elias Ashmole was initiated in 1646 the presiding officer was described as "Warden"; but with the example of the guilds before them there was apparently no difficulty in entrusting the rule to an elected Master who would appoint his Wardens and other officers, if any, and whose tenure of office could be limited – but this may have been a later development.

The wish to keep the modes of recognition secret would necessarily involve some sort of ceremony, thus leading to the development of ritual; but we know that the ritual developed over a period of years and it was a long time before anything like a standard version emerged; indeed we all know that even after the attempted standardisation following the Union of 1813 variations still occur; so even if we can accept the need for ritual as a landmark, the ritual itself cannot be one.

There is evidence which suggests that the operatives may have worked a two degree system and certainly the growth of a degree system was a very early development in speculative Freemasonry and it might perhaps on this basis not be unreasonable to consider for inclusion the existence of a hierarchy of degrees, or at least of two degrees, as a landmark, but for the fact that a third degree was later added.

We could go on testing one thing after another in this way and I do not propose to do more now than draw your attention to two more possible candidates for a list prepared on this view of our origins: the basis of the masonic system of morality as "brotherly love, relief and truth" – which I remind you includes toleration of the beliefs of others – and the teaching of that system by reference to allegory based on the working tools of the operatives and on the building of King Solomon's Temple.

There we must stop, not because these lists cover all possible candidates but because my objective is to get you thinking about something we profess to regard as important but, I dare to suggest, might have difficulty in explaining to a candidate or a critic, which can hardly be regarded as a plus point for the Order in general or for us and our lodges in particular. On the other hand, it would hardly be fair if I did not tell you that my personal belief about which items constitute "ancient landmarks" would be that there are four: first, belief in TGAOTU; second, the open VSL in Lodge; third, the recognition secrets and their sanctity; and fourth, brotherly love, relief and truth as the basis of our "system of morality".

This is put forward with some diffidence as it is to be hoped that your thoughts will concentrate on criteria rather than about whether this or that item should or should not be a landmark; there is something far more important than that at stake, and so we come to the final point I have to make to you, the real purpose of this paper.

We have seen that early origin and permanence are qualities which landmarks, at least if entitled to be termed "antient", must possess; but over a period of years social mores change and we are dealing already with a period of nearly three centuries to date. Many things which were important to our ancestors in the 17th century do not have the same value or relevance to our lives today while others survive from century to century. We cannot presume that future generations will accept our codes and practices in anything but basic morality and if Freemasonry is to prosper in the future, which as a social phenomenon it can only do if it is seen as relevant to the social environment of the time, it is vital that we should not encumber it with unneeded baggage. This is the reason for the question mark which you may have noticed at the end of the title of this paper. We have to preserve those things without which Freemasonry would not be itself, the landmarks, and any "established customs" which a Master is required to enforce in his lodge. But every extra item which we try to thrust into one of these categories will, if we succeed, be a hostage to the future and if in the future it ceases to be relevant or acceptable in changed or changing times, it will operate not as a preserver of the Craft but as a destroyer – mark that word, for it is deliberately chosen – a destroyer. At a time when so much is changing so quickly we do well to think of this if Freemasonry is to remain an effective force for good. Men will listen, as they always have, to myths and traditional stories for the lessons they so graphically teach; they will not listen to, will not even hear, or worse, will despise, outmoded irrelevancies. So I end as I began with a cautionary verse; you may feel that it contains a moral:

"It is a glorious thing to be
An omnipotent omniscient Lodge D.C.
What I don't know I invent,
And if challenged I observe
'It's an instant ancient Landmark
Which I'm anxious to preserve'."

3
The Templars and the Rose Croix
History and Myth in Freemasonry

Before the Union of 1813 which brought together the Premier Grand Lodge ("Moderns") and the Grand Lodge of the "Antients", Freemasonry had a basically christian orientation and though the "Moderns" only recognised the three craft degrees (excluding the Royal Arch), the "Antients" considered that any "masonic" degree could be conferred under the authority of a craft warrant. After the Union only the three craft degrees (including the Royal Arch) could be so conferred, though there was an exception for "Orders of Chivalry", and the Duke of Sussex, as Grand Master, supervised the removal from the ritual of christian references. This removal was attacked by some as changing an ancient landmark and many Provinces continued to attend church services before their annual meetings or such occasions as the laying of foundation stones.

A number of christian degrees and Orders had been practised prior to the Union under the craft warrant or by special authority. The most prominent and popular was probably that of Knights Templar. As is made clear in a subsequent paper, this was to give rise to trouble; but the exception in favour of the "Orders of Chivalry" was enough for the time being to satisfy the Brethren involved. However, the duke, who was Grand Master of the masonic Knights Templar, did nothing to promote it and it would seem to have declined in London at least. To understand later developments and how these Orders and Degrees developed in isolation from the Craft we must understand their origins and development.

Linked with this is the question of the power of myth and its place in Freemasonry, something which historical accuracy must not be allowed to denigrate.

The objective in this paper is to examine links between the United Orders – commonly called KT – on the one hand and on the other the degrees of the Ancient and Accepted Rite as it is practised in England, in particular the eighteenth or Rose Croix and the thirtieth or Ne Plus Ultra. To do this we shall have to study the origins of both Orders, but first there are some general points to make of which the most important is the difference between, and the relative values of history and myth.

It is a common saying that we should not believe everything we see in print, though it is even more of a commonplace that many people – too many – do just that. It is certainly true that we should not believe anything which we read or are told about masonic history unless we are fully satisfied that it is at least based on good factual evidence. This may seem obvious, but it is remarkable how gullible we are when we want to believe something. We should therefore first determine the kind of things we are likely to want to believe in this case.

The most important probably arises from a yearning for roots. There has been much publicity about this recently in many fields of which Freemasonry is only one; for example, the descendants of slaves searching for their origins; adopted children trying to trace their parents; or our own atavistic interest in family trees. The basis of all this will often be the wish to understand where we belong, how we fit in with the pattern of the universe and in particular to assert individual identities; but it can give rise to an obsession with the history of anything which interests us, particularly where social phenomena are involved; and Freemasonry is such a phenomenon. This in turn can bring into action a tendency so to interpret history as to make it more acceptable, what should have happened instead of what did, or even what a particular group want us to think did happen. History abounds with such cases; Shakespeare's plays Richard III and Macbeth are well-known examples.

This fascination with roots does not account for all our interest in origins. Curiosity, with which we are all endowed to a greater or lesser degree, can focus attention, and something casually read or heard can become embedded in the mind as fact, particularly if it has a romantic appeal or is put forward with an authority which convinces us of our own ignorance and perhaps offers the opportunity of showing off our newly-acquired knowledge. Interest so aroused is seldom critical until the alleged fact is challenged and even then the challenge may be ignored because if proved it would spoil the romance.

So much for dangers to researchers from their own predelictions or, more insidiously, from the motives of others. We must now tackle the difference between history and myth and the important step in this is to rid ourselves of the idea that a myth is simply an insubstantial fiction. In fact, it is often, in the words of an established theologian, an attempt to build "a framework in terms of which one could intelligibly relate to the world and respond to it". Myth is in fact often the first stage in man's efforts to establish his identity and importance in the face of the unknown. It has its place even in the sophisticated world of today, as we can see from the current obsession with cyberspace. It is important to ask why myth is accepted in this way even when it clearly clashes with historical fact. One reason is that it can motivate our subconscious minds. We may not believe in the reality of the Garden of Eden but the biblical stories of the Creation shaped the worship and framed the thoughts of our ancestors until the very recent past and may be hidden influences on their descendants today. Other biblical stories too can still have their hold on the subconscious minds even of those who challenge them: David and Goliath, Moses and Pharaoh, Jacob and the many-coloured coat, Noah and the Ark, and Noah and the rainbow for example. Other instances from our own history would be King Arthur and the Round Table, King Alfred and the cakes, King Canute and the waves. In modern times a terrifying example of the power of myth can be found in the National Socialist movement in Germany which brought about the holocaust and second world war.

For good or ill myth has its place in our lives just as history does and one of the problems confronting the researcher is the danger that his arguments and discoveries may cause others to reject long-cherished beliefs and leave their lives the poorer. The point here is that if you know or learn that something you have regarded as historical fact may be historically false and never have happened, you should not eject it out of hand as valueless. It may still be part – and as we shall see an important part – of the fabric from which our history and social mores have been spun and the probability is that it has survived because it has something to teach us. It has in fact become a part of history as part of the framework of the thoughts of our predecessors. It follows too that we must assess their actions in the light of their beliefs and be ready to learn from myth even when we doubt the historical accuracy of its content.

It is important to remember that history may provide us with facts but it is often the myth which supplies the inspiration and is the motivating force. To quote a theologian again, "The essential point can be put in terms of the contrast between a search for meaning and a search for history". I would not go so far as to agree with Henry Ford's famous remark that "History is the bunk", which is more a sound-bite than a definition, for after all if it were true we should not know who Henry Ford was; Ambrose Bierce may have been nearer the mark when, in The Devil's Dictionary he defined it as "an account, mostly false, of events mostly unimportant, which are brought about by rulers mostly knaves, and soldiers mostly fools", but that is more a warning than a definition. Antiquity is not always the guarantee of value which we tend to make it; myth on the other hand tends to present the lessons of the past in allegorical and generally more memorable form, history as it ought to have been rather than as it, usually unfortunately, was.

The parables of the christian gospels vividly show the power of this method of teaching; but it would have been pointless to try to pick out the Good Samaritan in documents of that time or to try to count statistically the amount of seed which fell by the wayside. We must not confuse the sign with what it signifies but follow its message if we are to get to the destination to which it points us.

This lengthy introduction is needed because of the interest aroused by some specious recent works about Freemasonry; they give the impression, which examination shows to be unsustainable, of being drawn from thorough research and documentation. This may sell books but it is not genuine scholarship; in fact it sometimes exploits the unfriendly interest in and suspicion of Freemasonry for the encouragement of which the Craft has only itself to blame. This blight has recently spread to accounts of the masonic Knights Templar, albeit at the would-be sympathetic hands of Freemasons; but that is only one manifestation of it. We shall come back to the specific case, but first we must ask what are the historical facts?

The first solid fact is basic to all research into the history of speculative Freemasonry, the establishment of the first Grand Lodge on St John the Baptist's day, 24th June 1717. Even so, we only know about that from hearsay as the earliest minutes we have are dated 24th June 1720, three years later; but it is generally agreed that the fact is proved. We can then work backwards from that date, but this is not the place in which to examine the early history of the Craft; what we must try to determine is whether there was in 1717 any history of previous association between on the one hand, Knights Templar, Rose Croix or Rosicrucian tenets and on the other, the Freemasonry of the new Grand Lodge. The answer has to be that we have no evidence which even suggests that there might be. The first attempt to formulate a connection seems to have been in about 1737, twenty years later when a Scot who had emigrated to France, the Chevalier Ramsay produced there his so-called Oration. It was probably never actually delivered in England though he made an English translation. He attributed the origin of Freemasonry to the knightly crusaders rather than to the operatives. The oration was widely circulated in the fourth decade of the 18th century in France, where lodges were being formed, probably as a result of the presence of Jacobites leaving England in the wake of the failure of the 1715 attempt to restore the Stuarts to the thrones of England and Scotland. This spread would have considerable influence on later developments as Gallic exuberance embroidered the more stolid Freemasonry of the British and the earnest elaborations of the Germans.

The Oration was eagerly seized upon as showing that the Templars had founded speculative Freemasonry, which was not what Ramsay had claimed but which very soon a great many people came to believe; here is an excellent example of the love of antiquity at work to create myth. The result was probably a boost for Freemasonry and so can be seen as beneficial but the fact remains that there is no evidence to support it and no known source from which Ramsay could reasonably have deduced any connection. However, we still have to ask ourselves how did the connection between the two Orders which we now have arise? To answer that, we must first look at the later history of the Templars.

The final eviction of the crusaders from Jerusalem in 1244 ended their original mission but the Templar Order continued to exist and grew so rich and powerful that it attracted the envy of religious and secular authorities. By the 14th century the French King was the most powerful monarch in western Europe. The papacy was the supreme spiritual power but was the centre of much corruption and the focus of much ambition. It was also a focus of concern for the temporal powers whose persuasive and sometimes forceful backing was essential for every occupant of St Peter's chair. In 1303 the forces of the king of France, Philip the Fair, had publicly stripped and degraded Pope Boniface VII and effectively brought about his death in squalor; the new pope, Benedict XI, died a year after his election amid rumours of foul play and Philip, who was determined to have a Frenchman amenable to his will on the throne of St Peter, acted promptly and with vigour. He made a scandalous deal with Bertrand de Grot, Bishop of Bordeaux, promising to support his candidacy on three conditions; in view of the fate of Boniface two years before it was hardly likely that the King's wishes would be ignored and Bertrand became Pope Clement V. Two of the conditions were known to him before his election but the third was sealed and only to be revealed if his candidature was successful. It proved to require the suppression of the Knights Templar. In 1312 a papal ballista or bull, as the formal decrees of the pontiff were called, was promulgated commanding the destruction of the knights and the confiscation of their property, much of which was to pass to the Knights Hospitaller, the Knights of St John of Jerusalem, an Order then based on Rhodes but whose origin also dated from the Crusades. The decree was eagerly obeyed in France although in many other countries of western Europe it seems to have been ignored. By torture, Philip extorted from the Grand Master, Jacques de Molay, and many of his knights confessions of abominable behaviour and of corruption and in 1314 de Molay and others were burnt at the stake. Many other Templars were murdered. As he was bound to the stake de Molay summoned Pope and King to confront him at Christ's tribunal; within a year, both had died.

It seems likely that individual Templars survived in several countries but the Order as such was effectively destroyed. There have however, been persistent claims that the Grand Mastership survived and one such legend links it with Scotland where Templar relics exist; but then they exist in England also, as in the round church in the Temple in London and similar buildings elsewhere, notably Cambridge and Northampton. There is also a document of very doubtful authenticity known as the Charter of Larminius which has been claimed as supporting these theories but which, in the opinion of the historian of the English masonic Order, Frederick Smyth, and of other historians, is either a forgery or relates to another Order. Nevertheless, a legend grew that some of the Templars escaped to Scotland, joined masonic lodges there and founded a new degree, called Kadosh, a Hebrew word which we shall meet again and which conveys an idea of holiness or sanctity; its supposed objectives were to recover the confiscated property and to kill all Knights Hospitaller; the name was later applied to a masonic Templar degree.

We do not know whence the masonic fascination with things Scottish comes, though the Jacobites in France must be a possibility; another such fable relates that on the completion of King Solomon's temple the masons who had been employed there gravitated to Scotland where they established lodges. There are good reasons for doubting all these stories, not least because we have no evidence of the existence of such lodges, and there is also the difficulty that the legends talk of places and give names the existence of which is not substantiated.

We now pass into the world of myth. While Freemasonry was expanding in many parts of the world in the latter part of the 18th century, considerable ingenuity was put into the fabrication of degrees, particularly by the French, who seem to have found the basic degrees lacking in flair; many of these degrees lasted only a very short time, but well into the mid-19th century Dr Oliver was still able to list about a thousand. In general, the degrees which were popular and survived where those related to some well-known story, character or event which gave them a vivid but illusory provenance and at least an appearance of antiquity. In the atmosphere of mid-18th century England this made the Bible a prolific source and episodes which could be strained into apparent relevance to operative masonry were specially popular; these included Noah's Ark, the Tower of Babel and above all King Solomon's Temple and later the second Temple. The Babylonian captivity was thus brought into the mix and before long the interest of inventors spread to the Christian era. The deeds of the crusaders brought in both

Templars and Hospitallers regardless of their alleged hostility and later the roman emperor Constantine the Great who ruled from 306 until his death in 337; he had made Christianity the official religion of the empire after a vision and had built Constantinople as his capital. Almost any story or legend could become the basis of a masonic degree and many did; among them was the degree of Knight Templar. At some point quite early in their history the masonic Knights Templar began to practise a Rosy Cross degree, sometimes wrongly referred to as rosicrucian, in addition to the kadosh degree.

Parallel with all this activity in the mid-18th century was the spread of Freemasonry to many other parts of the globe, often in the wake of military conquest and colonisation. Most important for our purposes were France and Germany. The Gallic exuberance of one Etienne (otherwise Stephen) Morin to whom in about 1761 the Grand Lodge of France granted a patent authorising him to promote Freemasonry throughout the world, produced a rite of 25 degrees in the French West Indies; it spread widely and is often referred to as the Rite of Perfection; it included a precursor of the Rose Croix degree. The harder-headed Germans invented the Rite of Strict Observance which has been suggested as the origin of the masonic Templar degree. So-called masonic degrees and orders proliferated without control.

Into this chaos stepped some shadowy figures of whom we know nothing. King Frederick the Great of Prussia had been initiated into Freemasonry at some time in the mid-18th century; he may later have ceased to be interested but in 1786 he was dying and shortly after his death a series of documents appeared which purported to have been issued by his authority as self-styled Protector of Masonry and to bear his signature which however, is said to bear no resemblance to any example accepted as genuine. Where the other signatures on the documents are still legible they are not those of anyone recognised as prominent in Freemasonry. Nevertheless, these documents, known as the Grand Constitutions of 1786 have ever since been accepted as forming the degrees of Morin's Rite and eight other degrees into a new rite of 33 degrees to be known as THE ANCIENT-ACCEPTED-SCOTTISH RITE of which the Rose Croix and a degree known as Sovereign Commanders and Sovereign Knights Kadosh became respectively the 18th and 30th. We have seen that "kadosh" is supposed to have had a special significance for the Templars so here is a reference to the masonic Templar tradition in an Order other than the Templars, who by the end of the 18th century were also practising a Rose Croix degree.

The new rite was intended to spread by the formation of Supreme Councils on a scale of one Council for each sovereign state, with certain modifications and exceptions, and as you know it has been established in many countries and is still spreading. In 1819 a patent for a Supreme Council in England was granted to the Duke of Sussex, first Grand Master of The United Grand Lodge of England and H. J. da Costa, but almost no action was taken under it. In 1845, two years after the duke's death, Dr Robert Thomas Crucefix obtained another patent, this time from the Supreme Council of the Northern Jurisdiction, USA, and that is the authority under which the Supreme Council in London now operates.

We have already noted the opinion that the masonic Knights Templar degree may have originated from the German Rite of Strict Observance. Certainly there is no proof of Scottish origin, and the earliest definitive reference to the installation of a masonic Knight Templar so far found is on 28 August 1769 in Boston, USA; this however, clearly implies an earlier, possibly much earlier, origin. The earliest such record in England is in October 1778 when Thomas Dunckerley advised a lodge in Portsmouth that they might make Knights Templar by virtue of their Craft warrant; the lodge worked under the Grand Lodge of the Antients which regarded a Craft warrant as authorising the working of other degrees. In fact the Articles of Union which founded The United Grand Lodge of England in 1813 expressly reserved the right of Craft lodges to confer degrees of chivalry, something which later was omitted from the published text.

Meanwhile, what of the Knights Hospitaller? After being expelled from Palestine they found their way eventually to Malta. The English division (or langue to use the technical term) withered when England became Protestant but the other langues continued in Valetta where in 1565 the Turkish army besieged them. After an heroic defence, the siege was raised and until the Napoleonic era the Hospitallers remained there, growing in power and wealth. In the 18th century there is evidence of masonic lodges on the island, in spite of the facts that the Order was limited to Roman Catholics and Freemasonry had been condemned by the popes. An Inquisitor was appointed and in April 1776 he began an enquiry specifically directed to exposing all past and present members of the Craft. In an article in the 1993 volume of AQC Bro Caywood describes how the records of this inquisition seem to have been effectively suppressed, perhaps because the Grand Master of the Hospitallers may himself have been a Freemason. Incidentally, Bro Caywood records details there about an Initiation which you might find of interest. There is however, no evidence so far as I am aware that Maltese Freemasonry had anything to do with other than the basic masonic degrees, and the origin of our Malta degree would appear once again to have been attributable to a romantic search for fresh material on which to found a masonic legend.

In 1798 the Hospitallers surrendered Malta to Napoleon Bonaparte. The knights were dispersed; some abandoned their vows but some where given imperial protection in Russia and eventually re-established the Order in Rome in 1834; this however, remained an Order bound to the Roman Catholic Church and so having nothing to do with Freemasonry. The masonic Malta degree became associated with the masonic Templar rite probably for no better reason than that the Templars and the Hospitallers were both military Orders, both dated from the crusades and both offered an air of romance and history – myth at work again. In this way the United Orders came into being, a strange phenomenon which defies traditional history by bringing together two Orders one of which, according to masonic tradition, had vowed to exterminate the other. The apparent contradiction has never been explained and indeed it cannot be because when Freemasons adopted the trappings of both they could not claim true historical descent from either.

We now come to one of the books to which I referred earlier, *The Templars and the Lodge* by Baigent and Leigh. It elaborates the theme of an earlier book by the same authors and Henry Lincoln, *The Holy Blood and the Holy Grail.* It propounds the theory that the Knights Templar in Scotland survived the papal bull and were involved in the origins of speculative Freemasonry and the founding of the Premier Grand Lodge in 1717. However, the authors write "if there was a connection between the Templars and the 'operative' stonemasons in Scotland, it would, in any case, have exhausted itself by the 15th century". Nevertheless, by way of John Dee and others, they claim that the Templars were responsible for the founding of speculative Freemasonry. The alleged evidence for this has not been found acceptable by scholars and you can find detailed criticisms in reviews by Bro Jackson in AQC 94, and somewhat astringently, Bro Gilbert in AQC 101. The most that can be said is that the authors are surely correct in thinking that the pot-pourri of "hermeticism, alchemy, sacred geometry and all the teachings and traditions which had originated in Alexandria during the first, second and third centuries [A.D.] had their part in setting the stage for the emergence of Freemasonry"; but this is only true in the limited sense that all those things, and many others, contributed to the general flowering of philosophic thought and analytical thinking which blossomed at the Restoration and formed, in my view, the background against which speculative Freemasonry came into being.

We advance now to the Union of the two English Grand Lodges in 1813. Contemporary records indicate that masonic Templar Encampments were meeting regularly and that in them four degrees were being conferred: Knight Templar, Knight of Malta (including the Mediterranean Pass), Rose Croix and Ne Plus Ultra, a rough translation of this being "let there be nothing higher". It seems probable, though by no means certain, that Templary was particularly strong in the West Country and perhaps in the North. But 20 years after the Union it was losing ground in London. In 1834 Dr Crucefix, who, you will remember, was later responsible for obtaining a patent for an English Supreme Council, founded the Freemason's Quarterly Review and used it for various purposes, one of which was to promote the masonic Templar Order, including the Rose Croix and Ne Plus Ultra. The third number appeared in October 1834 and contained references to the masonic Templars and to the original Knights Templar and a correspondent was assured "the [masonic] Knights Templar are not forgotten". Subsequent numbers contained further references and it would seem that Crucefix tried to rally the London Encampments into making a joint protest to the Grand Master about failure to hold a meeting of the ruling body, the Grand Conclave. The Grand Master had since 1812 been the Duke of Sussex who had already, as we have seen, prevented the establishing here of the Ancient and Accepted Scottish Rite and seems to have been in no hurry to promote the masonic Knights Templar whom he nevertheless professed to admire. He did not relish the pressures which Crucefix was bringing to bear in various causes, and matters came to a head in 1840 when an attempt to expel Crucefix from the Craft narrowly failed.

After the patent to form a Supreme Council had been granted to Crucefix in 1845 he and his successors proceeded cautiously with negotiations to get the Rose Croix and Ne Plus Ultra degrees recognised as exclusively the province of the Ancient and Accepted Rite. You can read about their progress in the recently published official history *Ancient and Accepted.* It was some time before the Templars were prepared to accept the claim and even today both Orders are combined in the Baldwyn Rite in Bristol – but that is another story. The two degrees are now firmly established as the province of the Ancient and Accepted Rite here, in which they form the 18th and 30th degrees.

We must now examine this tangled skein to see what lessons we can learn from it. I suggest there are two. First, a possible conflict has been averted and the original high principles of the Templars, from which, by the time of their suppression, they had so sadly fallen short, were revived – myth at work again for our benefit. Second, and perhaps more important, the Ancient and Accepted Rite in England and Wales and throughout the jurisdiction of its Supreme Council has remained true to the ancient Christian tradition which it has inherited with the English Rose Croix and Ne Plus Ultra degrees now incorporated in it, and which date from years before 1786, when the degrees which now form the Ancient and Accepted Rite were brought together. This Christian condition has been the subject of comment by some Supreme Councils, most of which are now what we term universal and did not understand the background, a misunderstanding which has hopefully been remedied at the 1995 Lausanne Conference of Supreme Councils. In fact, omitting the special case of the Scandinavian countries, only under the Supreme Councils for England and Wales, Scotland, Ireland, Finland, Australia and New Zealand is the Rite exclusively Christian.

Because of the origin of its two principal degrees, the Supreme Council in London, whose jurisdiction presently extends to the control of more than 800 Chapters at home and overseas, thus regards itself as the successor to the masonic Knights Templar who once controlled the equivalent of those degrees. This association is not unique; the Supreme Council of the Northern Jurisdiction of the USA, who granted the patent to Dr Crucefix, at one time required that candidates for the 18th degree must have been installed as Knights Templar before they could be Perfected. However, what is probably not capable of explanation is how we can reconcile the presence in the United Orders of both Templar and Hospitaller traditions with the masonic tradition of hostility between the two. Suffice it to say that members of the United Orders wear the trappings of both and support the hospital at Jerusalem which is the successor of that founded by the Hospitallers so many centuries ago, and that any animosity from the past has been expunged by the masonic tradition of brotherly love.

PART TWO
BREAKING THE MOULD

The two Grand Lodges whose quarrels had marred the second half of the 18th century were united in 1813 to form The United Grand Lodge of England with HRH. the Duke of Sussex as Grand Master, a post he retained until his death in 1843. His exclusion of references to Christianity from the new rituals, his increasingly autocratic conduct (though the forms of democratic government were preserved), his studied inaction in relation to the masonic Knights Templar together with the administrative problems arising from the increasing incompetency of one of the Grand Secretaries, Edwards Harper and the complaisancy of a clique who formed the core of the Grand Lodge inevitably produced demands for reform, muted at first but increasingly strident. Enter Dr Robert Thomas Crucefix. Himself an efficient administrator, he put forward proposals for reform; his energy on behalf of the charities led him to take up the proposals for an "Asylum for the Aged and Decayed Freemason" and eventually into open conflict with the Grand Master. In this imbroglio Dr George Oliver, D.D., the most respected masonic author of the time became involved. The results were to affect English Freemasonry for the rest of the century.

In this part, Oliver and Crucefix are studied, the nature of the world in which they lived is remembered, their contribution to the development of the Craft is assessed and the events which eventually settled the exclusion from the Craft of everything except the three degrees and the Royal Arch are detailed.

4
George Oliver, D.D. 1782-1867

After the Union of 1813 the Duke of Sussex dominated English Freemasonry as a benevolent autocrat. However, reform was in the air and new men were everywhere coming to the fore as wealth came to many whose forebears had known only modest standards of life. The franchise was extended in spite of entrenched opposition. In Freemasonry too unrest was felt. Those who were in comfortable authority were complaisant and there were ominous signs that in London at least membership was falling. There was also unrest about the apparent official neglect of the Knights Templar; and the removal of Christian references and allusions in the ritual still rankled. There was little communication between rulers and ruled and energetic Deputy Provincial Grand Masters such as George Oliver were rare. Grand Lodge minutes were only published after long delays. It was only a matter of time before protests would appear.

The duke began to go blind with cataracts. He continued to govern and direct but was increasingly dependent on his entourage for information. Before his sight could be restored in an operation Dr Robert Thomas Crucefix had begun campaigns to reform the administration. In this he gained the support of the Rev George Oliver, D.D. who was becoming known and revered widely as a masonic author. The tension rose and the effects would reshape Freemasonry as well as producing a reaction restricting publicity about the Order. To understand how this happened the personality and beliefs of these two men must be understood. This paper studies Dr Oliver.

George Oliver, the "sage and historian of Masonry" was born 5th November 1782 and was ordained as a priest in the Church of England in 1814. He remained an active parish priest until 1855 and until his death faithfully served his Heavenly Master. That statement is deliberately phrased to stress at the outset that in spite of his great love for Freemasonry and his glowing reputation among most of his masonic contemporaries he could not have found the tenets and principles of the Craft acceptable had they not been reconciled in his mind with the religion which was his life and hope; but it also means that we must consider what was the accepted orthodoxy of theological thinking at the time when his thoughts were crystalising, because he was of course a creature of his time, and theology, like all social sciences, is continually developing.

It was an important part of the Christian faith as commonly understood in England in the 18th century and well into the 19th that the Bible contained the revealed will of God and that everything in it, from the creation stories of Genesis to the visions of the Book of Revelation, was literal and unshakable truth; men might dispute whether Adam and Eve had worn fig-leaves or breeches, but not the fact of their creation, which was confidently asserted to have occurred in 4004

BC. Satan and Hell were as real as the Pope and Roman Catholics and for many Englishmen there was a marked similarity between all four.

In George Oliver's long life the world of Dr Johnson would give way to that of Jane Austen and he was destined to live on into that of Trollope; steam, electricity and gas would begin to transform transport, communications, work and domestic conditions; commerce would bring new goods to market from abroad; man would dangerously begin to believe himself master of the universe in his own right rather than because he had been created in the image of God; and towards the end of the period the whole theory of creation, and the authority of the Bible, would be challenged by Charles Darwin when *The Origin of Species* was published in 1859.

As to the stock from which he came, Bro Dixon, writing about 25 years after Oliver's death, justifiably attributes the eminent masonic career of the son in great measure to the example of Samuel Oliver, his father, a preacher and teacher who had been initiated into Freemasonry on 12 July 1797 in St John's Lodge, Leicester. Dixon, quoting "one who well remembers him later in life" describes him as "a host in himself, full of anecdotes and reminiscences of a long career, thoroughly appreciating his glass and long pipe and the good things of this life, extremely fond of a joke, yet withall a God-fearing man". The picture which emerges from this and various references in *The Freemason's Quarterly Review* is of a down-to-earth, practical man, physically strong, mentally alert, a good companion, a devoted pastor and a keen mason.

With such a background it is not surprising that George Oliver became interested in Freemasonry as a youth and when a new lodge was formed in Peterborough in 1802 of which his father was to be chaplain though the city was 20 miles from their home at Whaplode, he put himself forward as a candidate.

It would seem that the new lodge was originally set up in July 1802 to work under the Antients' Grand Lodge but apostatised, obtaining a warrant from the "Moderns" on 23rd December. The precise date of George's initiation is not known. He was not yet 21 but this was overcome, perhaps by a dispensation (though none has survived) and it would seem that because of his minority he took his obligation with his father kneeling beside him as his guarantor – a somewhat unusual procedure of which both the origin and the legality are debatable. It seems that he must have been unable to attend the Lodge often for in 1803 he took up a post as Assistant Master at a school in Caistor, 25 miles north-east of Lincoln. He had apparently already served some time in an attorney's office in Holbeach. He does tell us however, that he was Passed and Raised in Peterborough.

In 1805 he married Mary Ann Beverley, some six years his elder. There were five children of the marriage: George, Caroline Burnett, Beverley, Charles Wellington and Mary Pierpont. In 1809 he was elected Headmaster of the Freemen's Grammar School at Great Grimsby and feeling himself now settled in a career (though he later lamented that his income was dependent "upon the caprice of Individuals who . . . are not wholly to be depended on") he lost no time in resuming his Freemasonry. In 1811 he founded Apollo Lodge on a purchased warrant and set about the building of a masonic hall, where (as he later confessed) he spent much time in solitude, planning the course of his masonic studies and working out the beginnings of a masonic philosophy.

He was ordained priest in 1814 and at once appointed curate of Grimsby and vicar of nearby Clee. The incumbent at Grimsby was Dr Tennyson, father of Alfred Tennyson, later to become Poet Laureate, and brother of Charles who later, presumably because of his friendship with the Grand Master, HRH the Duke of Sussex, became Provincial Grand Master for Lincolnshire and appointed Oliver as his Deputy.

In a farewell sermon preached at Grimsby in 1831 Oliver vividly described the condition in which he found the church building when he was appointed and typically eulogised the state in which he was leaving it: "I found the fabric damp, dirty and forlorn, without casements in the windows for a free ventilation; the windows themselves in the last stages of decay; the walls green from the effects of moisture, and the floor wet . . . no public charity . . . no Organ; no tunable bells . . . Opposed to this melancholy picture, look at the state of the place now . . . You have a beautiful Church, clean, dry, and perfectly ventilated . . .The churchyard I planted out at my own expense."

Notwithstanding the clerical duties he had undertaken, he remained headmaster of the school until 1826.

He had been exalted into the Royal Arch in Hull on 8th May 1813, and may possibly have been received into other Orders there. In 1823 the first of his many masonic publications appeared, *The Antiquities of Freemasonry.* Over the remaining 44 years of his life he would publish many more.

His curacy at Grimsby ended with the death of Dr Tennyson in 1831 and to his chagrin he was not offered the living; nor did the new incumbent, with whom he soon fell out, wish to retain him as curate. The bishop came to his rescue, appointing him to the rural living of Scopwick, a "secluded village" 12 miles south of Lincoln. It was not the best of livings but he was fortunate to find one. Dixon describes the village at that time as "in such a state as to be a proverb and a by-word among the neighbouring villages" but indicates that Oliver put all to rights in a few years and *Scopwickiana*, written by Oliver in 1837 paints a much happier picture.

To return to masonic matters, Charles Tennyson had been appointed Provincial Grand Master in November 1832. In 1835 he assumed the additional name of D'Eyncourt by which he was thereafter generally known and which we must now use. In October 1833 he appointed Oliver as his Deputy, a post which in those days often carried the duty of day-to-day administration of a Province; indeed, until dismissed in 1842 Oliver virtually ran it. There was at the time of his appointment scarcely an efficient lodge in the Province and he started by making new appointments to offices which, in many cases, had been held by the same individual for many years. A new and determined broom had arrived and a new, prosperous era for the Province was swept in.

In 1834 Oliver, who was feeling the loss of corn rent income at Scopwick, was appointed additionally to the charge of the Collegiate Church at Wolverhampton, then a royal peculiar in the gift of the Dean of Windsor. In 1835, aged 52, he was awarded a Lambeth doctorate in divinity, probably for certain publications in defence of the Church of England. But then things began to go wrong. The growing town of Wolverhampton may well have considered itself too grand to be a mere fief of Windsor. There were blazing rows between Oliver and his churchwardens and Oliver, who seems to feel he had been let down by the deal, infuriated the bishop by threatening to offer the position to the highest bidder. The resignation of the churchwardens led to an uneasy peace but Oliver still lived for part of the year at Scopwick and his curates at Wolverhampton were a continual source of trouble. The whole system was in need of reform and the death of the dean in 1846 was the signal for parliamentary action; Oliver and the rector of South Hykeham, near Lincoln, exchanged pulpits in 1847. It is clear that he, with his firm view of the duties and powers of an incumbent, had been the wrong man to be head of the ecclesiastical establishment of such an independently minded town at that stage of its growth.

No sooner had the initial uneasy truce at Wolverhampton been achieved than trouble began on the Lincolnshire masonic front. To understand this we must look back to 1834 in London. Bro Robert Thomas Crucefix, a doctor with a substantial practice, adequate fortune and a strong supporter of masonic charity, began to champion the cause of "the aged and decayed Freemason". The boys' and girls' institutions were well established and a benevolent fund tried to meet the wants of the needy, for whom there was of course no welfare safety net. There was however no machinery for looking after those who were no longer able to earn a living, could not afford a home and were forced to choose between the workhouse and abject poverty. Crucefix espoused their cause and began to lead a campaign to raise money to build an "Asylum" for them. The Grand Master, who was always both sensitive about the dignity of his position and jealous of his authority, not unreasonably felt that he had not been properly consulted in this and made his opposition known. Crucefix, who in 1834 and without applying for official approval (on the grounds, as he later admitted, that it would not be forthcoming) had begun the publication of a quarterly magazine, *The Freemason's Quarterly Review*; he used the magazine to circulate masonic news and to promote the cause of the Asylum. The Grand Master disapproved of both but many Masons supported Crucefix and feelings ran high. D'Eyncourt had supported the magazine at first but on learning of the duke's disapproval withdrew his approval. Oliver had also supported it and he continued to do so. Later, D'Eyncourt publicly approved a determined effort to expel Crucefix from the Craft.

Meanwhile, Oliver and Crucefix, who had first met in 1839, had become fast friends and when, after the failed attempt at expulsion, a number of his supporters decided to present a testimonial to Crucefix at a masonic dinner in

London which was well publicised, Oliver agreed to preside and make the presentation; this action greatly displeased the duke who left D'Eyncourt in no doubt about his views. D'Eyncourt, who had already refused Oliver's proffered resignation, hummed, hawed and hesitated but on 28th April 1842, when he was expecting the duke as a house guest, he wrote to Oliver summarily dismissing him as his Deputy. Oliver was furious at what he considered the discourteous and insulting manner of his dismissal and the Province, which adored him, was in uproar. The indignation spread far beyond Lincolnshire for Oliver was well-known and appreciated as a masonic writer and Crucefix was not averse to fanning the flames. Matters were eventually patched up with D'Eyncourt just before the duke died in 1843. On 9th May 1844, after a very public campaign, a testimonial was presented to Oliver in his turn at a banquet; this was held in Lincoln as Oliver, who periodically had qualms about his health, did not feel equal to the journey to London which Crucefix, ever the showman, would have preferred.

Oliver had continually been producing books and pamphlets about Freemasonry and they had won him a reputation at home and in many countries overseas as – in a phrase apparently coined by Crucefix – "the sage and historian of Masonry". Among other honours he accepted the rank of Past Deputy Grand Master of the Grand Lodge of Massachusetts in 1845 and in the same year was approved by the Supreme Council of the Ancient and Accepted Scottish Rite for the Northern Masonic Jurisdiction of the USA as Lieutenant Grand Commander to Crucefix in the patent for a new Supreme Council in London; indeed, it would seem that his appointment was a condition for the grant of the patent as the sponsors had apparently some doubts about whether Crucefix could be trusted to support some of their policies about external relations. For a brief period after Crucefix's death in 1850 Oliver was Sovereign Grand Commander and regularly described himself therafter as "Past S.G.C." in spite of his short and somewhat contentious tenure of that office.

At the age of 72 Oliver's voice began to fail and he seems to have entrusted parochial duties to curates. He finally retired from Scopwick and South Hykeham in 1865. His wife had died in 1856. He made a farewell appearance at Lincolnshire Provincial Grand Lodge in 1866 and died in Lincoln on 3rd March 1867 after a short illness.

With that introduction we can now briefly consider his prolific masonic publications which of course reflect what was then the traditional view of Freemasonry and of its origins. That view is important because, largely due to Oliver's elaborations and explanations and the popularity of his work, it continued to represent masonic orthodoxy long after scholars had challenged or refuted much of its conclusions. More than 60 works by him were published, about half of them on masonic subjects. It is clearly impossible to mention them all within the confines of one paper and only those of major importance to our understanding of him can be covered. A full bibliography can be found in the biography *Priest and Freemason.*

He gives two accounts of why he began to write about Freemasonry. In one he says that the incident which first set him to the task was too trivial to be recorded and that his earlier masonic works were "intended, in a great measure, for his own private amusement"; in the other he refers to the bitter mortification of being unprepared to refute arguments against the Order and attributes this inability to the fact that masonic literature was then very circumscribed, and extended information difficult to obtain – matters which it is important to remember in judging his work.

In later years he more than once refers to a plan he formed early in his masonic career a "Grand Design" for a cycle of works which would constitute a detailed view of the comprehensive system of knowledge, human and divine, which for him was Freemasonry. The foundation was laid by the publication of *The Antiquities of Freemasonry* in 1823 and *Star in the East* in 1825, respectively designed to show the antiquity of the Order and to establish that it was in essence Christian. In 1826 he wrote about masonic terms and technicalities in *Signs and Symbols* which was dedicated "by permission" to the Duke of Sussex. Next he investigated initiation rites in *The History of Initiation* (1829); then a volume with the astonishing title of *The Theocratic Principles of Freemasonry* was published in 1839 to show "the true philosophy of the Order". In 1845 and 1846 respectively he published the two volumes of *The Historical Landmarks of Freemasonry,* in which he examined at length the course of what he considered to be Freemasonry from the beginning of the world. The work is a tribute to his capacity for extensive reading and to his retentive memory and may have been largely responsible for the charge of credulity later levelled against him.

Because of "frequent and particular enquiries" about ceremonial and usage *The Book of the Lodge* appeared in 1849, describing in detail how in his view a lodge should be conducted and lodge premises be built and furnished. Then in 1850 he published what he described as the cope-stone of the Grand Design; this was *The Symbol of Glory.* In it he wrote "I have endeavoured to redeem the Order from the charge of frivolity which was brought against it in the last century, by showing its applicability to many of the sciences – I have portrayed its literary character – I have pointed out the various sorts of amusement and instruction of which it is the author and dispenser; and in this, my closing work, I have shown how, in concurrence with other causes, its sincere professors, through the merits of the Great Architect of the Universe, may find their way to another and better world".

Remains of Early Masonic Writers, published in five volumes between 1847 and 1850 was a collection of 18th century masonic writings and has a distinctly pro-Christian bias; Oliver made so many footnotes as almost to convert it into another original work. *Revelations of a Square* (1855) was based on his father's papers collated to form a narrative of the progress of an imaginary 18th century lodge. *The Freemason's Treasury* (1863) contains "52 lectures . . . adapted for delivery in Open Lodge". It was published, says Oliver, because "all our Worshipful Masters are not eloquent nor do the most fluent speakers always make the best rulers of a Lodge of Masons". To this we might add "Right, Most

Excellent, in every particular". In 1886 he wrote a pamphlet on papal teachings in answer to a papal bull which condemned Freemasonry; in it he generously offers to clear the Pontiff's mind "from the doubts and uncertainties which have led him into error" – a pompous and presumptuous statement which was hardly likely to further his cause.

Just before he died *The Origin of the Royal Arch* was published; he considered the Order to be "a fabrication of this country" originating about 1740, something more reasonable than his further suggestion, made on insufficient and probably inaccurate evidence, that the Chevalier Ramsey might have had a hand in it.

Now, if Oliver's writings are to be objectively assessed, we must examine what he understood Freemasonry to be, why he wrote about it, and how his acceptance of it was allied to his firm and unshakable religious belief. Like Preston before him, he believed Freemasonry to have existed from the beginning of the world. This belief is in sharp contrast to almost all modern theories, which may of course themselves be wrong. The argument would run thus: God created the universe; human beings were created in God's image; it was to them that God revealed his purpose, and with one race of them that He later made His covenant; the early books of the Bible show that His plan for that part of the human race which He had chosen as His own is all-embracing, governing every facet of their lives; therefore there is an all-embracing rule of conduct for them which has been in existence from before the Creation and has gradually been worked out for them in revelation and history as humankind has come more and more to understand God's purpose or as that purpose has been gradually revealed. That purpose reached its fruition in the coming of Christ, the Messiah, and the giving of the new covenant. A new system of morality and conduct thereby grew from the old, and it again embraces everything necessary for carrying out God's will for humanity; this system does not purport to provide the rules for religious celebration or to dictate dogma, but concentrates on what we must do in our daily lives on earth, how we must behave – a handmaid in fact to religion. Freemasonry is exactly that and is in fact the embodiment of that system. Therefore Freemasonry is that system and has existed, even if only gradually revealed, from the Creation.

Few will accept that reasoning today but if it is how Oliver, in keeping with his time, reasoned, then it is in the light of that belief that we must assess his work.

The main reasons why he wrote about Freemasonry seem to have been, first, his belief that inadequate information about the Craft was available to its members, and second, his view that it was necessary to answer publicly opinions which charged that Freemasonry was inconsistent with Christian beliefs and "show clearly to what religion, if any, the present system of Masonry was analogous" which, in *The Star in the East* (1825) he had proved to his own satisfaction was Christianity; he wrote "It is much to be lamented that the casuistry of the present day should be used to sever the connection between Freemasonry and Religion. It arises out of the mistaken notion that Freemasonry entertains the ambition of superseding religion altogether; which is as wide of the truth as the poles are asunder . . . It is not in itself religion; but the handmaid and assistant to religion. It is a system of morality, inculcated on scientific principles, and morality is not the groundwork, but the result and fruit of religion."

How then could he accept the presence of non-Christians in lodge? He reminded us that God Himself had promulgated the doctrine of the brotherhood of man and wrote "No matter what may be the birth, language or colour of the skin, every man is a brother if he faithfully performs his duty to God, his neighbour, and himself". He was equally firm with those of his clerical brethren who doubted the propriety of allowing their churches to be used for masonic occasions and in this connection produced one of his more memorable aphorisms: "It is freely conceded that Freemasonry is not Christianity. Neither is the Church of England."

Four things prevented his views from harsh dogmatism. First, although in defending the Christian religion he is outspoken and forthright, he is at no point uncivil, or unkind, even to those who have attacked him. Second, although by nature something of a fundamentalist he recognised and applauded scientific progress saying "while the world moves on in an uninterrupted course of improvement, Freemasonry must not stand aside; for if she hesitates ever so little – time will pass, and she will be distanced in the race".

The third point is the importance he placed on the lectures and particularly on keeping their content up to date. In his view conducting the monthly lecture was a duty which the Master must perform; each lodge meeting should include some amplification of masonic principle and precept; he wrote "I entertain a very indifferent opinion of a Master who works in his Lodge solely by the tenacity of his memory . . . He is only a machine . . . I have known Masters who could repeat the whole of the three lectures by rote, and yet were entirely ignorant of Masonry."

The final point which kept him from dogmatism was his view on what could at that time genuinely claim to be Freemasonry. In 1846, after listing 941 degrees in 44 rites he limits the system to "the symbolical degrees, the Royal Arch and Templary"; the last-named would at that time have included the Rose Croix.

A Century of Aphorisms (1849) sums up much of his practical masonic teaching. The best known (and sometimes least regarded) is the statement that great numbers are not always beneficial; others include: one who despises the hour of refreshment is . . . a hypocrite, formalist or impostor; the great excellence of the system lies in the happy distribution of history, science, morals and metaphysics in the lectures; "he is a wise Brother who knows how to conclude a speech"; the remedy for subduing turbulence and restoring harmony in a Lodge is to dismiss the Master. There is also one which shows him as the child of the 18th century in more than his philosophy: "A young Mason should never pretend to a knowledge which can only be gained by experience. The higher the ape climbs, the more effectually he exposes his posterior deficiencies."

How then did his contemporaries view him? The Lincolnshire brethren knew him best and basked in his reflected glory as the "sage and historian of Masonry";

they also loved him. Following his dismissal in April 1842 the Province was in open revolt and at least one resolution of no confidence in the Provincial Grand Master was carried. In making a presentation to him in Witham Lodge the spokesman said "However much we esteem his learning, however highly we might esteem his talent, our feelings would be cold indeed compared to what they really are, had he not, in every relation of life, under all vicissitudes, and under every circumstance, shown himself not only to be influenced, but controlled by the purest principles of Masonry". A less sympathetic opinion in a letter in the Grimsby Public Library refers to him as "a great antiquary and yet a small one. Immense in facts yet quite unable to do justice to them . . . But there was a thorough kindly simplicity what made everyone like him." A writer in *The Freemason's Quarterly Review* wrote that "his style of public speaking is quiet, deliberate and persuasive, attended with inflexions or intonations of voice, and a little subdued action. His sermons are written in a plain and simple style . . . Brother he is to all Masons and friend he is to the world." He said of himself "By nature humble and unassuming, it is difficult to draw me out for the purpose of lionising" – apparently an accurate statement though he did on occasion sound his own trumpet with vigour. An obituary in the *Stamford Mercury* read in part "in dignified retirement, honoured and beloved . . . He was of a kindly disposition, charitable in the highest sense of the word, 'thinking no evil', courteous, affable, self-denying and beneficent, humble, unassuming and unaffected; ever ready to oblige, easy to approach, amiable, yet firm in the right."

How should we assess him today? Freemasonry is only one part of a man's life; Oliver's masonic virtues and vices, his abilities and his faults, cannot be considered in isolation. He was essentially, primarily, and at all times a Christian priest and it may well be that the urgency of his need to reconcile his religion with his passion for the teachings of Freemasonry made him uncritical in his wide reading and prone to draw conclusions that would fit his thesis; but he was able to bolster that thesis with impressive authorities both classical and modern. His research was certainly extensive; no-one who reads the books of the Grand Design or peruses the footnotes to the works he edited can doubt that. The marvel is how a country parson, not given to travel, zealous in his parochial work, "the recluse of Scopwick" as he was once called, could find the material he must have searched out or have had the time to absorb it when found. If, as both Kenning and Dixon claim, his writings effectively started serious historical research into Freemasonry, that in itself was an achievement of considerable merit; he himself said "I conceive that I have merely opened the mine".

The progressive rejection of much of the religious and masonic traditions in which he had been brought up and the sheer bulk of his writings have conspired to sink his works into oblivion, emerging only when some critic with the advantage of the fruits of more than a century of masonic research in an age of easier communication and with more sophisticated tools has taken his work off the shelf, given him a good spanking for failing to live in the 20th century and put them back to gather dust; but that is not a verdict on him as priest, man or mason. As a priest, we have a picture of sincerity, struggle and often achievement. As a man we know much to his credit and little to his harm. As a Mason he revived and united a Province and effectually governed it for nine years during which he was respected and popular: the two do not always go hand in hand. In precept and writings he upheld a tradition of sound and orderly working in Lodge and gained a world-wide reputation as an expert on ceremonial and usage. He became a legend in his lifetime and lodges and chapters in many places have been named after him. He made enemies in high places but that was the fault of sincerity and his wish to promulgate the principles of Freemasonry too publicly for the masonic establishment. He probably wrote too much and was undeniably prone to accept what he read as accurate without keen investigation – but travel and communication were not then as simple as they are now. In the history of masonic research he may be criticised but he was a pioneer in the field and cannot be ignored, if only because of the influence he wielded and the effects of which would still be felt long after his death.

He tried to meet three challenges: to show that Freemasonry was supportive of and compatible with the christian religion, to convince the world of the value of Freemasonry as a system of morality, and to ensure that in an age when both were advancing fast, masonic teaching kept pace with scientific and technological progress lest the Craft should be seen as an irrelevant survival from a bygone age. A century and a half after his death the Craft in England is beginning tentatively to confront the first two; it may soon have to consider the third. The problems which Oliver faced remain today and if we are to meet them we may well learn from one who did not shrink from the challenge.

5
George Oliver's Scopwick

We have moved so far from the agriculture-based world of the early 18th century that it is difficult sometimes to appreciate how the emphasis of life and its pace have changed. This paper is included as a reminder of the very different world in which Oliver and his contempories in the country outside London mostly lived.

Sometime in the early 19th century the vicar of a small Lincolnshire country parish read an article in Blackwood's Magazine in which the author expressed surprise that clergymen did not write accounts of the life of their parishes and of the lives of their parishoners. He was a scholarly man and a writer, but above all else he was a pastor; his name was George Oliver and at the time when he is introduced to us he was 55 years old, very active and not without knowledge of the world and its ways, though in no sense could he be called worldy. Born in 1782 he had in 1809 been elected headmaster of the Freemen's School at Grimsby; there he wrote two pamphlets on education of which one only seems to have survived; it shows him to be enlightened in advance of the times on such issues as the need to teach the poor and the means to that end. It was written in about 1846 as a direct result of his experiences in Wolverhampton which was in the throes of the Industrial Revolution.

In 1814 he had been ordained a priest in the Church of England, and instituted as vicar of Clee, the 'Clee' of Cleethorpes, and appointed curate of Grimsby, where he found the church neglected, damp and dirty. When, 15 years later, the death of his patron, Dr George Clayton Tennyson, deprived him of the curacy he left behind him a church in good repair with a numerous and lively congregation which would apparently (at least according to him) have wished him to get the living. Dr Tennyson was a pluralist who held other, more attractive livings and was content to leave Grimsby to his curate; he was the father of Alfred Tennyson, later Poet Laureate, and had a brother Charles with whom Oliver became very friendly.

Oliver was particularly interested in archaeology and antiquities, read a great deal and had a very retentive memory. He believed implicitly in the literal truth of the Bible and accepted Archbishop Ussher's chronology which placed the creation of the world in 4004 BC. This was of course the accepted orthodox wisdom of his time. He was strict where his vocation was concerned and not above claiming credit for himself where he felt it was due. But above all, and in spite of a generally retiring disposition except where his livelihood was concerned, he had the ability to gain the affection and confidence of his fellows in all walks of life. Without means or connections and in a harshly practical world he nevertheless attracted the attention and interest of two successive bishops, the Dean of Windsor, and the Tennyson family. He was awarded a Lambeth Doctorate of Divinity at the age of 52, probably for a reply to a recently published essay on corruption in the Church of England. Pictures of him at that time show a resolute, clear-eyed man, healthy, and confident. He was happily married with three sons and two daughters. Later in life – he died at the age of 84 – portraits show a spare figure, bespectacled, with the look of learning and an indefinable expression in which authority and affability are mixed in what I think must be the air which our forefathers, using the word in its true sense and not with its cynical modern meaning, called complaisant.

Such was the man who was appointed in 1831 by the Bishop of Lincoln to be vicar of Scopwick, a village of some 300 inhabitants, between Lincoln and Sleaford. He retained the living until 1867 though for the last ten years or so of his incumbency he employed a curate to carry out most of the duties. As the corn rents which formed a major part of his income decreased he sought additional work, for which he has been derided as a pluralist holding more than one living at a time, though the record shows that he worked hard at both. From 1814 to 1846 he was thus in charge of the Collegiate Church in Wolverhampton, then a Royal Peculiar, to which he had been nominated by the Dean of Windsor who was also Dean of Wolverhampton as a result of a historical quirk and a royal whim.

Wolverhampton was a fast-growing industrial town and the demands which its squalor, dirt and moral degeneracy made on Oliver seem to have made his time in charge of the spiritual health of the parish unhappy and made him miserable. He later mitigated this by employing a curate. But although he was busy, the Blackwood article intrigued him. He loved writing and had already published several pamphlets and four books on antiquities and churches which had attracted considerable attention, and several articles in the Gentleman's magazine. In 1838 he took up the challenge of the author of the article and produced *Scopwickiana, or Sketches and Illustrations of a Secluded Village in Lincolnshire*, a small booklet of some 65 octavo pages in which he described the village and its life. It was typical of his inability to control his pen once he started writing that the finished work proved too long for the magazine.

Scopwick, which the inhabitants called "Scawby", lies 12 miles south of Lincoln and eight miles north of Sleaford. It is today an attractive place, lying off the major road, which passes by to the west. Almost the whole of the village lies along one street which runs parallel to a small stream whose banks form a sort of village green and across which a number of small bridges give access to houses on the south side. Another road, parallel to the village street and to the north of it gives access to a small number of houses of which one was in Oliver's time the vicarage. The village has no particular artistic merit but is simply a quiet Lincolnshire village in a pleasant setting away from the traffic of the main road.

Writing in 1894, 56 years later, another Lincolnshire author describes it as being at the time of Oliver's arrival, "in such a state as to be a by-word amongst the neighbouring villages. No school nor school-room; the church walls and floor covered with green moss, from which drops of water trickled continuously; scarcely any congregation; the churchyard wall in a ruinous condition; and the vicarage houses and premises uninhabitable". Oliver had never considered the duties of a parish priest to be limited to the holding of services and visiting the sick and he set about improving matters immediately and with such vigour that when he wrote *Scopwickiana* seven years after his arrival he was able to paint a very different picture and an article written about him in *The Freemason's Magazine* in 1840 was able to state "He has a well-filled church of attentive hearers who are partial to his ministry". By then also a schoolroom had been provided. In *Scopwickiana* he refers to one of his improvements, the rebuilding of the vicarage. With an acceptance of the social conditions of the time which takes our modern breath away he wrote: "The old Rectory and Vicarage were low, damp habitations, unfit for human residence; with rooms five or six feet in height, and altogether destitute of convenience. The former is inhabited by servants[!]; and the latter has been replaced by a new stone house of moderate dimensions." It consisted "simply" – that is Oliver's word – of dining and drawing rooms, two kitchens and five bedrooms (which he calls "sleeping apartments") with "the customary offices"; his sons and daughters would all be at home at the time when he wrote. The rebuilding was apparently done at his own expense, a proof of the success he had thus far achieved, probably largely from his writings for he was becoming known as a masonic author of daunting ability and high purpose in addition to his books on antiquities.

Of the remainder of the buildings in the village, he wrote: "little can be said and that little is anything but satisfactory". Some of the villagers' cottages in fact consisted of only one room about 12 feet by 10 feet in dimension, open to the thatch, and many of them were so close to the stream that they were flooded when it overflowed, which was a frequent occurrence in times of rainy weather, being fed by plentiful springs; in consequence ague and rheumatism abounded. Not surprisingly, in view of his energetic enthusiasm, plans were afoot for rebuilding, plans in which he and then squire, Charles Chaplin of Blankney, seem to have been jointly concerned.

The population of the village in 1838 is given by Oliver as 321, broken down as follows:

Vicar	1
Farmers	5
Cottagers	7
Tradesmen	15 of whom Oliver says nothing
Labourers	35
Children	95 almost equally divided between sexes
Hired servants	52
Adult females	111

The working life of the village revolved around the local farms and Oliver draws a picture of surprisingly contented existence. It is probable that he saw more of content than discontent because he himself appears to have been what today we would call a charismatic character; but the personality of the squire, Mr Chaplin, probably helped.

Of approximately 3,500 acres of farmland round the village, 2,760 belonged to the squire who also held leases on a further 500 acres vested in the bishop. Chaplin's attitude was therefore bound to have a dominant effect on the villagers and it was fortunate that he seems to have been a very enlightened man for his time. He had given to each labourer in the village a rood of land to cultivate, sufficient to grow a year's supply of vegetables and enough potatoes to feed a pig, so that each, with (Oliver notes) one or two improvident exceptions, had a pig in the sty and flitches of bacon in the chimney corner. The squire also allowed his employees to buy loppings from fir-trees in his plantations cheaply for fuel; these were locally known as "kids" and there were consequently "kid-stacks" on the stream banks as winter drew near.

The labourers were basically agricultural workers – very quiet, sober and provident, Oliver tells us. They would have three or four miles to walk to their work in the morning and in the evening would spend a couple of hours or so on their rood of ground, Chaplin having prudently reckoned that a rood was all they could work without impinging on the time they would need for his work. The wages were 12 shillings a week – say about £50 at today's prices, with two "strikes" of malt a year and the privilege of working by the acre during harvest. A strike was a local measure which varied from place to place and could be anything from one to four bushels – a bushel is usually taken to have been eight gallons. Oliver, who admittedly was sometimes naive, commented that though the patience and good-feeling of the majority in discharging their "most onerous duties" was beyond praise, yet in the world in general "few would work unless compelled to by the goad of necessity".

The focus of the year's activities was of course the harvest. A cycle was generally observed – turnips drilled in with bones, barley, seeds and wheat. Oats and beans were not considered profitable and so were only grown for individual consumption. Some dairy and farmyard produce was marketed and a cylindrical cheese was produced and consumed in the village; Oliver thought it would have a good sale if marketed, being in his view "superior to the Stilton". The usual poultry, plus peacocks, were bred for sale though peacocks were not greatly esteemed – something that may seem odd since peacock as a meat has been, and still is, esteemed a great delicacy in many parts of the world.

When harvest time came round the labourer would rise at three o'clock and, with his wife and children under 14, go to the cornfields. The men sheared or mowed; the wives bound the sheaves with bands made by the children. Work lasted for 16 hours with "infectious cheerfulness prevailing" in view of the extra money being earned which made the difference between a bare existence and a modest living. For an industrious family gleaning could provide seven or eight strikes of wheat and enough barley to feed the pig; this was mainly women's work and was not the only job they did on the farm for others came with the seasons, such as picking out stones before ploughing for there was sufficient loose limestone just below the surface to ruin a crop if it was not got away. Children started work at the age of six "tenting birds" and gradually worked up to more serious jobs until at 14 they were considered old enough to "take a place" (as the phrase was) and from then on their parents were considered as relieved of the duty to maintain them. Life was hard and revolved around the basic needs for living.

A great deal of the labour consisted of yearly hirings of both men and women. The hirings were from old May Day and were arranged at "statute fairs" held in all large towns and many villages. In Scopwick this period was preceded in the houses of the hirers by several violent weeks of spring-cleaning, which Oliver regarded as a sort of personal purgatory. The justification for this was partly to get the most out of the servants who would be off to the statute fair thereafter and partly to ensure that the house would look attractive to those who would be hired to replace them and on the principle that if they came to a tidy, clean house hopefully they would realise that it must be kept so. The newly-hired could indeed repent of their bargain at any time before taking up their new employment by returning the "fessen penny", anything from one to five shillings given to bind the hiring contract; or the new employer could cancel it before it was taken up by allowing the employee to keep the fessen penny.

Statute fairs were the scene of much jollification and considerable licence was allowed; fights often developed and linchpins might be removed from carriages. An unpopular employer might hear an unfavourable view of his character bawled out by erstwhile employees. But no employer could refuse his employee permission to attend up to two such fairs a year unless he had accepted a fessen penny.

In Scopwick the morning of a nearby statute fair would be marked by early visits made to neighbours by mothers taking young daughters to receive their good wishes for success at the fair. The girls would go off in best bib and tucker, the young men would wear slop frocks in blue or white, each with a badge in the hat to denote the wearer's trade: a lock of wool for the shepherd, a thrum of whipcord for the waggoner, a bunch of horsehair for the groom.

Quarrels between servants were generally left over for settling at the statue fair; once the fair was over, battle would be joined. For those without scores to settle, a general parade of the streets by the girls would soon attract the young men and the fairs were in fact looked upon as something of a marriage market. The parade would end with dancing at the various public hostelries, dances which Oliver describes as "performed with agility, skill and toil; for it appears that they strive to please their lovers more by muscular exertion than by graceful movements".

Sometimes courting at these dances would be rudely interrupted. One way of starting mischief was for an onlooker to throw a handful of nut shells at a girl, saying something like "You'll throw nutshells where your love lies, hoi reckon". This was nearly always good for a fight in which the whole room would soon be embroiled. Then clothes were put to rights, blood washed off and dancing resumed as if nothing had happened.

There was (and is) a public house in Scopwick, the Royal Oak, kept by a woman whom Oliver, with obvious approval called "a widow of the old school". No spirits or wine were sold, only ale, and a man who called for more than two or three pints at a sitting was liable to be packed off home with the words "Your wife wants you" or "You've sat long enough and I'm fond of fresh faces; so go at once". She was 74 years old and had only been out of the parish three or four times, going not more than 20 miles away and not happy until she could return; but such was her rule that Oliver notes "No Temperance Societies are wanted here".

On St Thomas's day and Shrove Tuesday the women of Scopwick went out "goodying". Dressed in all the rags they could muster they would march through the village as if, in Oliver's words, "all the maukins in the parish had deserted their station in the cornfields". Thus attired, they would ask everywhere for gifts in cash or kind. It was a way of sharing goods to enable the poorest families to get through the winter without loss of face.

But surprisingly happy though Oliver's general picture of his village is, he takes to task those who idealise the cottager's life as compared with that of the gentry. "Comparative felicity may be attained," he says, "such a thing is possible; but positive felicity is inconsistent with this imperfect state" and referring to one noble poetess he derides "her want of experience in those humble scenes to which she so enthusiastically refers". There were in fact not unnaturally murmurings and discontent and he quotes the lament to him of an intelligent labourer's wife that "if the rich were as unkind to the poor, as the poor are to each other, nothing could save their families from absolute destitution".

In a generally orderly community there is often a disorderly element. In Scopwick this was provided by the large proportion of hired labourers and servants. Oliver not unnaturally put at the head of their crimes that they – or at any rate the men – clearly did not consider themselves as in any way duty bound to reverence the parson and to some degree would influence the young village lads by their conduct. It particularly upset him that they persisted in profaning the Sabbath by playing "chuck-penny" which consisted of throwing halfpennies into a hole, the man who was successful then collecting all the coins that had been thrown, tossing them up and keeping those that fell head uppermost.

Other games were in vogue too, but with the Inclosure customs had changed. The garlanded maypole was no longer put on the church tower early on Mayday morning, nor later on the green. Ploughs were no longer drawn along the village street on Plough Monday – the Monday next after the Epiphany – a ceremony that was complicated by efforts to entangle someone in the ropes and drop him into the stream, which was where the whole party usually finished up anyway. Cock-fighting had ceased; formerly it had been an annual event in a field behind the church, and the pit still remained. Bonfires and dancing on the green had stopped. Only football survived and the young men played it on Sunday to the chagrin of their vicar. However, one public holiday was still kept, with ass races, foot races for men and for women, sack races, wheeling a barrow to a given point blindfolded, and so on. This all took place on the land of Squire Chaplin, who provided the prizes. Oliver laments that the most constant winner habitually took all his prize money to the beer-shop.

Another custom abandoned since the Inclosure was that of beating the parish bounds. The old method of doing this had been for a procession of elders and boys to visit a number of the holes which marked the boundaries and make the boys stand on their heads at each to impress on the brains, in more ways than one, where the parish boundary ran, a method so successful that Oliver records that many of the old men distinctly recalled exactly where the holes had been.

The great festival in the village was Holy Cross Day, the patronal festival. Hospitality was then by custom extended to all members of one's family not living in the village. Plaster floors would be whitewashed and decorated in black with a composition of soot and water to imitate a carpet. There would be much scrubbing and scouring and provisions were laid in against the expected invasion. Squire Chaplin helped by making a general distribution of game, usually a hare for each family. On the day itself droves of visitors would arrive and the children would be given money and packed off to the gingerbread stalls which the travelling fair-people had by this time set up with other entertainments, the day being a regular fixture in their calendar. In the houses, after the usual enquiries, gossip and exchange of family news visitors and hosts settled down to a meal which would be followed by a general parade round the village for more gossip and the renewal of old acquaintance.

It is clear that however old-fashioned this may seem to us today times were changing fast. Oliver refers to several abandoned customs such as the May-day celebrations; these had begun on the previous evening with drinking "possets of frumenty" in one of the cottages and the making of garlands to adorn the houses on the day itself; garlands would also be made for the maypole to be set up on the church tower at dawn. In the afternoon another maypole would be set up on the village green but before that the milkmaids had danced and sung their way to the common, "their pails or piggons being dressed with flowers", the first to reach the common being dubbed "Lady of the Common" for the day.

Dancing round the maypole in the afternoon had been a lively and boisterous business. There had also been other activities on Mayday of which Oliver mentions "duck under the water Kit" as a favourite; he does not explain it except to say that the lads and lasses performed it with great glee the whole of the distance to the nearby village of Kirby Green and back "augmented on their return by the rustic population of that village". As the villages are some four or five miles apart this must have used up a great deal of no doubt surplus energy.

Oliver paints a charming picture of one character in particular: Nelly Smalley was over 90 years old and in his words "a poor harmless creature that is a general favourite". On Sunday she would be in church, dressed in a grey serge cloak with a little bonnet tied on with a black ribbon, the very picture of devotion, "her really benevolent countenance beaming with edification and piety". But outside the church she was an incessant and compulsive talker, her voice was monotonous and to save time she tended to leave out the shorter words in her conversation, saying such things as "it rain", "it tunner" or "it dirty". She was the self-appointed and unofficial messenger of the village and would cheerfully take messages and light parcels round the countryside for the villagers; there she unfailing delivered, but in her own time and as she was a popular character well-known over the surrounding area and constitutionally incapable of passing a house without calling in for a chat the delivery process could take some time; but, as she said, "they think behave ill, if pass wi'out callin" . . .

Nelly had a small pension from "the Union" – the poor law authority, of course, not the modern version; and in addition to her self-imposed work as messenger she supplemented it by such expedients as gathering cowslips for any families that wanted them for wine-making. For clothing she relied on gifts of old bonnets, shoes and the like. Oliver says, and here I quote him directly again, "Nothing is so truly pleasing as to confer a favour on poor Nell. There is a freshness about her way of returning thanks, so unstudied – so familiar, yet so touching, that I have always thought the giver is the most gratified person . . . nine or ten shillings is a little fortune to her; or, as she herself terms it, "a nice bit o' money"; and it is of more service than the thousands annually expended by the prodigal".

There is much more, for George Oliver was as observant as he was profuse in explanation. I have tried to select enough from *Scopwickiana* to give the flavour of a small Lincolnshire village in the aftermath of the Inclosures and before the pull of industrial wages and the slump in agriculture made their marks. It is essentially a parochial picture in every sense; few of the villagers would normally go further afield than Lincoln or Sleaford, and then only under the pressure of economic need. Their lives were hard and not many would have had a living much above subsistence level had it not been for a benevolent and thoughtful squire. That they were quick to appreciate those who sincerely tried to help them is clear from the way they reacted to Oliver's care for them, attending church where formerly they had rarely done so, and greeting him in the street and in their cottages cheerfully and with regard.

Oliver himself was aware of the problems of life on an inadequate income, albeit one which would seem luxury to the villagers he strove to serve, and had a lively concern for their problems. He hoped for better things for them in the future, saying "there really exists much murmuring and discontent – much of ingratitude for favours received, amongst the working classes" – and here we should remember that he was also concerned at this time with welfare and education in the squalors of Wolverhampton. He goes on to hope, in keeping with his calling, that with the blessing of God the discontent may be removed for the next generation by mental culture. Alas, what mental culture was to achieve would be the two nation syndrome which still haunts us today.

In 1850, at the age of 68 Oliver was convinced that his health was failing and that it was time to hand over the care of his parish to a curate but the villagers persuaded him to remain. Five years later however he did feel unable to continue to be responsible for their welfare and on 25th March 1855 this gold old man, against whose character, as far as I have discovered, only one man had spoken – and he a charlatan – preached his last sermon in the village to which he had so devoted a major part of his life. In it is this passage:

> 'I have been preaching the gospel to you, my Brethren,
> faithfully and sincerely these many years, until my physical
> powers are exhausted; and as I cannot continue to discharge
> the duties of the Church with satisfaction to myself or benefit
> to you, I reverentially conclude that it is the will of my Divine
> Master that I should no longer abide with you."

Oliver died in Lincoln, poor but beloved and revered, on 3rd March 1867.

6
Robert Thomas Crucefix 1788-1850

Robert Thomas Crucefix was a man of great ability, persuasive, forceful and determined. He was essentially a crusader and those who came under his spell were soon his devoted followers, while others disliked or feared him with a similar intensity. His crusades for greater openness in Freemasonry and a refuge for those whom age, sickness or poverty had stricken were waged with a determination which opposition merely fostered and he was not afraid to take on the Grand Master, HRH the Duke of Sussex himself when he had either to do so or abandon the fight. Like many enthusiasts he could be blind to pitfalls, though he was far from being short of worldly wisdom. He achieved a great part of his mission but was probably largely responsible for the opposition to a more open attitude which characterised the long Grand Mastership of the duke's successor, the second Earl of Zetland who held the office from 1844 to 1870.

To condense the career of so turbulent a character into the space of one paper must necessarily result in painting with a broad brush. Those who would wish for further information may find it in Bro Jackson's history *Rose Croix* and my biography of Dr Oliver, *Priest and Freemason* and will also find much to interest them in the magazine he started in 1834, *The Freemason's Quarterly Review*, or, so far as the character, finances, learning and matrimonial tangles of the duke is concerned in Roger Fulford's delightful book *The Royal Princes*.

Crucefix was in fact one of those rampaging characters to whose activities others are compelled to react, in support or opposition, with greater force than their normal indolence would dictate. He has been compared to Samuel Pickwick and certainly could behave with the bland charm and naive affection of that gentleman and like him could involve himself and others who fell beneath his spell in unexpected complications. But there was also something of Napoleon Bonaparte in his makeup so that where the activities of Mr Pickwick accorded well with the small print of a novel, Crucefix's exploits often demanded headlines and bold type.

Here it is only possible to give a broad outline of his career; further details can be found in Ars Quatuor Coronatorum for 1989 pages 134-6. Born in London in 1788, he was at Merchant Taylor's School between the ages of 13 and 15 and then seems to have studied medicine. We know that he was at St Bartholomew's Hospital, London, as a pupil of its surgeon Ludford Harvey from 1809 to 1810 and became a member of the Royal College of Surgeons on 6th July 1810. He is reputed to have travelled to India but was back in London in 1814 in which year he married a widow; there were apparently no issue but he, his wife, his brother and brother-in-law, nephew and niece seem to have formed a close-knit and happy family. He apparently wrote several books on medical subjects but only one seems to have survived, *Time versus Life*, the third edition of which was published in 1844 and will be referred to later.

In 1829 at the age of 39 he was initiated into Freemasonry in the Burlington Lodge, London (now number 96) and joined Bank of England Lodge (which has no connection with the Treasury's city office) and was its Senior Warden in the following year. In 1831 he was exalted into the Royal Arch in Chapter of Fidelity number 3 and also joined Lodge of Peace and Harmony (now number 60), an important step because it is one of the lodges entitled to nominate a Grand Steward each year and in 1832, being also Master of the Bank of England Lodge, he was not only a Grand Steward, four years after being initiated, but was appointed to the Board of General Purposes ("BGP") and to the Board of Finance, becoming vice-president of the former in 1835. He was however, passed over for the mastership of Peace and Harmony and resigned from it in dudgeon shortly afterwards.

He was also becoming involved in other Orders, in particular the Knights Templar to which he was admitted in Scotland in 1831, receiving the Rose Croix and Ne Plus Ultra degrees, both then administered by the masonic Knights Templars, in England in the following year. In 1835 he was made an honorary member of Trinosophes Lodge in France, a well-respected lodge whose reputation had spread far beyond its native Paris; in 1845 he was made a Past Grand Warden of the Grand Lodge of Massachusetts. He had obtained Grand Rank in England as Senior Deacon in the Craft and Grand Standard Bearer in Supreme Grand Chapter in 1836 at the age of 47, nearly eight years after his initiation. He did not so much climb the masonic ladder as scale it with the rapidity of an assault.

Soon after his initiation he had become involved with the masonic charities and by 1834 was on committees of both girls' and boys' schools. He was also keenly interested in administration and seems to have suspected all was not well in the Grand Secretaries' office. His motives were rarely simple and were certainly suspect in some quarters; but although a new member he succeeded in extending the membership of both the Board of Finance and the BGP by the addition of a quota of elected Past Masters to each, thus ensuring a more representative membership. He also set about forming a Masters' and Past Masters' Dining Club, to meet before the Quarterly Communications of Grand Lodge which were then held at seven o'clock in the evening; as the Grand Officers met similarly and were briefed on the agenda by the Grand Secretary after dinner (a process which often delayed the opening of Grand Lodge), Crucefix's efforts could be, and probably were seen in some quarters as an endeavour to enlarge the scope of debate and a challenge to the establishment, which then meant the Duke of Sussex. There were, as he himself appreciated, those who regarded the comfortable status quo as something not to be disturbed.

For two further reasons 1834 was an important year for him; he founded, without prior approval, *The Freemason's Quarterly Magazine* (*FQR*) which he edited until 1846, and he became chairman of a project for building An Asylum for the Aged and Decayed Freemason. Both were to bring him into abrasive trouble with Sussex. He must have appreciated that exception might be taken to publication of the magazine for he later said that he had not sought permission because it might be refused; but when one considers that the minutes of the Quarterly Communications were often not published for months and that few Provincial Grand Masters attended them, anything that increased communication would be welcome to the average member however unacceptable any publication relating to proceedings in Grand Lodge or indeed any lodge might be to the masonic establishment.

The Asylum project was eventually approved by Grand Lodge in spite of a message from the duke, who was not present, urging that it should be rejected, a message which Crucefix, who had received no prior warning about it turned on its head in a masterly display of oratory; but the Duke persisted in his disapproval and after a turbulent meeting, to which we must return later, Crucefix and others were suspended by Grand Lodge and later an attempt was made to expel him.

We must now return to 1834 and *FQR*. In England Sussex was not only head of the Craft and Royal Arch but also of the Knights Templar; he also held a Patent authorising him to form a Supreme Council of the Ancient and Accepted Rite; in both these spheres he had been deliberately inactive; his reasons for this inactivity have been variously explained, the most plausible being that he did not wish the union so carefully crafted in 1813 and the removal of Christian references from the ritual which he had then insisted upon to be challenged by the growth of christian masonic orders. This inactivity was resented by many members of the Knights Templar order and Crucefix showed in early numbers of *FQR* that he intended to press for action, though he refrained from too open rebellion on this point so long as the duke was alive. But on the matter of the Asylum he would not hold his peace and in other spheres also he made his presence felt, achieving the investigation into the Grand Secretaries' office which he had sought and the resulting retirement of Thomas Harper, the former Grand Secretary of the "Antients" and who had held the same office jointly with W. H. White since the Union.

Whether all this activity was wholly disinterested is a matter to be considered but before doing so we must look at other material factors, of which the chief is the character of the Grand Master.

HRH Prince Augustus Frederick, Duke of Sussex

Augustus Frederick was the sixth son and ninth child of King George III. Freemasons tend to see him as a just but authoritarian Grand Master but if they do forget that Freemasonry was only a part of his life, non-masons do not seem to understand how important the Craft was to him. The rebellious temperament of a younger son, combined with an unsuccessful and officially invalid marriage, poor health and a recurrent lack of cash may well have created in him a basic insecurity which only a forceful assertion of his position would assuage and which Crucefix and his followers would ignore at their peril. He was very intelligent, interested in comparative religion, popular – too popular at times for the peace of mind of the government – with a strong sense of his position and not over-popular with his family, none of whom were his equal in intelligence.

In about 1836 a contemporary described him thus:

> " . . . a man of superior talents. It were to overstate his abilities to say he is a first-rate but . . . his intellectual resources are above mediocrity. [His] speeches were . . . remarkable for the ardent love of liberty which they breathed throughout . . . He excels in putting obvious truths into a popular form . . . he makes his views as clear to others as they are to his own mind. No-one yet mistook the drift of his argument . . . There is as much sense in what he says in ten minutes, as there is in what the majority of speakers would communicate in 20 . . . Everyone is struck . . . with the personal appearance of the Illustrious Duke. He is one of the tallest and stoutest men . . . in the country. He dresses plainly. Usually he wears a blue coat, light waistcoat, and light knee inexpressibles . . . His countenance beams with good nature, and with simplicity and sincerity of mind. There is something peculiarly "jolly" in his appearance . . . His face, like his person, is large and full, his cheeks are particularly prominent, and he has what is called a double chin. His complexion is something between dark and sallow, and his hair is of a brown colour."

He found the principles of the Craft, which he seems to have joined with a strong sense of its moral values, as congenial to his progressive, egalitarian outlook as to both his highly developed sense of his own position as a king's son (latterly very near the throne) and his liking for autocratic power wielded with a firm but generally courteous hand. In his latter years he grew less tolerant and more prone to listen to advisers who were anxious to please him and to secure their own positions; such activities as those of Crucefix and his friends in opposing his wishes in regard to the Asylum and the publication of reports in *FQR* about masonic matters which he considered to be private, were recurring annoyances to him which were bound to bring about an eventual explosion.

In 1832 he began to go blind. The trouble was cataract and the onset was rapid. An operation to remove the cataracts was possible but was accounted dangerous and in any case could not be performed until they had hardened.

When Crucefix published the first number of FQR in 1834 he included a guarantee of anonymity to contributors, an indication that he expected the project to be unwelcome to masonic authority. From its earliest numbers it supported the Asylum project, "the poor old Mason's cause", which the Grand Master had declined to approve. A further source of annoyance to him would be the prominence the magazine gave to and its comments on the administration of, the Knights Templar, including the Rose Croix degree which, in the void created by the duke's failure to act upon the patent to form a Supreme Council of the Ancient and Accepted Scottish Rite which he held, was practised in the Knights Templar Encampments. It would be a further source of annoyance that the magazine soon began to publicise the Masters and Past Masters Club of which it wrote in the number for October 1834 "Its object, if we are correct, is likely to ensure a regular attendance at the Quarterly Communications, by which any business thereat transacted will not only be more amply discussed, but more generally known throughout the Order". This was "Crucefix-speak" for saying that he hoped the Club would help to further such projects as the Asylum and not allow the "establishment" to sweep unwelcome proposals under the carpet of the Grand Temple.

It has to be remembered that at the time when the magazine made its first appearance the Grand Master's sight was rapidly deteriorating and by the end of 1834 he would have to rely on informers in order to learn what was happening. It was not long before he began to show signs of an annoyance which may have resulted from pique but was fostered on the one hand by Crucefix's ruthless insensibility in pursuing the Asylum project and treating the duke's constant "No" as meaning "Maybe" and on the other by a campaign of character assassination against Crucefix which developed among those who resented his prominence and the threat he represented to the cosy masonic world which had developed following the traumas which had preceded the Union and in which they enjoyed an easy and undemanding prestige. Material for this campaign was easily found in their victim's medical practice of which a substantial part was concerned with sexual disorders and diseases, and in his misfortunes in regard to a proposal for a masonic life assurance company, both of which we must now consider.

In the *FQR* obituary for Crucefix Bro John Lane gives almost no detail of his medical career, saying with infuriating detachment "Of the events antecedent to his initiation much might be written that would be interesting; but this is more a biography of the Mason than the man." However, some information can be gleaned from a broadsheet circulated by his opponents in August 1840 and the book *Time versus Life* already mentioned.

The broadsheet was issued by a Bro I. O. Truman, only recently initiated into Freemasonry, and was vicious even by the outspoken standards of those times. The allegations fall under the following heads:

1. Denigration of *FQR*.
2. A detailed attack on Crucefix's conduct as a medical man with thinly veiled suggestions that the basis of his practice was the treatment of venereal disease: that in short he was in the argot of the time "a pox doctor", and that he had an indirect interest in a patent medicine business for the treatment of (inter alia) sexual disorders.
3. Sneers at his conduct in Grand Lodge.
4. Allegations that he was making personal attacks on the honour of the Grand Master.
5. Suggestions that he was motivated by "petty intrigues or low ambition" to take control of Grand Lodge or split the Craft.

6. Criticism of the Asylum as "a masonic workhouse" – a slur which was later extended into suggestions that the project was not put forward for charitable reasons but to allow the promoters to make personal profits.

Little of value can be gathered from such venom except perhaps that Crucefix was possessed of such ability, energy and single-minded determination that one had either to like or loath him. The book however, is more illuminating though clearly its author would be biased in his own favour. The third edition was published in 1844 and apparently was not his only published work though it alone seems to have survived. It was a comprehensive and readable discussion of the natural deterioration and decay of human beings and a blunt analysis of the factors that might expedite the process. A copy is in the library of The United Grand Lodge. The book deals in detail with malfunctions of the human digestive tract and reproductive system in both sexes and makes it clear that the treatment of sexual diseases and disorders did form part of Crucefix's practice; but it also makes clear not only that he had a pragmatic approach to his profession and had considerable success in it, but also that he took psychological as well as physical aspects of a patient's problems into account and he quotes one instance in which a patient, discussing his son, read with approval moral precepts from a book which had in fact been written by Crucefix.

A few extracts from *Time versus Life* will illustrate its tone:

> "I have purposely avoided charging the present section of *Time versus Life* with the discussion of a particular class of disease to which the man of pleasure is subject. When *Time* permits, I may probably give the result of no common experience on a subject on which *Life* is so materially involved."
> "From obvious motives of delicacy, I have scarcely adverted to the dangers and difficulties which beset WOMAN, in her transit through *Life*. But I also propose, *Time* permitting, to consider of the subject, and point out the advantages of early "moral command".
> "It is just possible that the fastidious reader may question the propriety of appending to this treatise a class of disorders which are the sequels of indiscretion . . . The world should be looked at more as it really is than as it ought to be. "

Any campaign of character assassination could clearly make capital out of such a book and Crucefix's success in treating such disorders. As to the allegations that he was actively involved in a patent medicine business, it is not possible to make a judgement without more evidence, which is hardly likely to be forthcoming; but if true it would be a further proof of the fact that to him the end could justify the means regardless of man-made restrictions; the only caveat would be that for him the means had to accord with the dictates of the christian religion.

Dealing now with the life assurance matter, this appears to relate to a scheme in the original idea for which Crucefix was concerned and which would involve making insurance cover available for Freemasons on a basis which would favour the less wealthy. Others adopted the proposal, which clearly would require careful consideration if indeed it was practicable. Later, when the campaign against Crucefix began to take shape the allegation was made that he had intended to obtain personal advantage from the funds. Dr Oliver, a well-known author on masonic matters, DPGM of Lincolnshire and a firm friend of his, later voiced the opinion that it was this allegation which turned "the ruling powers of the Order" against Crucefix; after studying such information as is available I would not agree, feeling, as will appear, that the reason for official opposition to him was deeper and this rumour was only one part of a studied campaign to disgrace him.

The story of his involvement in the project sufficiently appears from an open letter to Bro R. W. Jennings from Bro John Lee Stevens in *FQR* for March 1840 from which it appears that Crucefix had agreed to become secretary of a company which was to promote the scheme, and deal with its correspondence, but had felt that the work would take so much time that the post should be a paid appointment. The letter alleged that Jennings had publicly stated that the project had originally been based on a "principle" which was to allow Crucefix to make a secret profit from its funds. Stevens commented: "The hypothesis . . . is as discreditable to your reasoning faculty, if you have any, as the conclusion is to your feelings" and pointed out that Crucefix had never been a director of the company but it had been agreed that the correspondence of the company should be expressly entrusted to him, for dealing with which he would be suitably remunerated, Jennings in fact asking him to come to a definite understanding on the question. Stevens ends by saying that Crucefix did not withdraw from the company in pique, as Jennings had suggested, but that Jennings refused to invite him to attend meetings of the promoters. Crucefix was, at the time, being subjected to much abuse which seems to have been orchestrated; Jennings may have been persuaded to join the traducers.

So much for the background. We can now resume the narrative.

In 1834 Crucefix became the leader of a committee formed to raise funds for building "the Asylum for the Aged and Decayed Freemason" and a theatrical entertainment in aid of it was held in London on 29 May 1835. None of this had been sanctioned by the Grand Master but a Bro Bell was deputed to write to seek his approval. The Grand Secretary replied that the Grand Master would "have much pleasure in fixing a date for receiving [a deputation . . . but His Royal Highness is desirous, before he does so, to be informed of the outline of the plan for the proposed Asylum, that is, the immediate objects of the Institution and the proposed or expected means for carrying the measure into effect, as well as for its permanent support."

Some information was supplied but the Grand Master did not consider it sufficient. Nevertheless, and in spite of a warning from the Deputy Grand Master and a letter from the Grand Secretary pointing out that masonic meetings held without the Grand Master's approval were illegal – which probably stretched the meaning of the prohibition – Crucefix continued to give the Asylum project publicity in *FQR*. The Grand Master continued to oppose it but vacillated in his reasons, finally saying that a building was not required and that a scheme of annuities would be preferable; no doubt he was influenced by expense recently required to remedy serious structural defects at the Girls' School. Nevertheless Crucefix stated his intention of proposing motions in favour of the Asylum at the Quarterly Communication in September 1837; he was "abruptly informed as Grand Lodge met that the Grand Master was opposed to the measure". He abandoned his intention but at the next Communication (December) Grand Lodge did pass a motion (confirmed in March 1838) recommending "the contemplated Asylum . . . to the favourable consideration of the Craft". By August 1839 the rulers of the Craft were being forced into a position where it could become impossible to halt the project with dignity and the duke decided to make a stand. He wrote a letter to the promoters, including Crucefix, and required the Grand Secretary to summon them and read the letter to them personally with a view "to avoid all further mis-statements and misapprehensions". The final paragraph was explicit:

> "Now, without imputing motives to anyone, there can be no doubt the Craft will be misled in supposing that I have given a silent consent to such a plan, which I am equally determined, as before, to resist; therefore, unless it is clearly understood that the intention of erecting an Asylum is totally abandoned, I feel myself under the necessity of declining any communication upon the subject."

The Asylum committee prepared a long and detailed rebuttal which was approved by a majority of subscribers on 13th November at a meeting which was far from orderly. Before it began an anonymous paper entitled "THE ASYLUM FOR WORTHY AND DECAYED FREEMASONS, ALIAS THE WORKHOUSE QUESTION" was circulated. It descended almost at once into personal attack, referring to the promoters as "Job Humbug & Co . . . every man jack of them seeking a Masonic contract which will put solid pudding into their own hungry stomachs and send the real claimants . . . empty away" and as "smooth tongued adventurers who speak of paupers and mean themselves". There followed a reference to "cunningly devised resolutions which give the lie direct to our Worshipful Grand Master, and seem to have been drawn up with a sly view of insulting him out of the Craft" to make way for an adventurer – an obvious reference to Crucefix.

A Bro Jackson, initiated the previous May and raised in August, was then identified as the author. A Board of General Purposes report found that "Various Calumniating Expressions were at that meeting publicly uttered by Bro Thomas Wood, Alderman, and Bro John Lee Stevens against our M.W. and Illustrious Grand Master and that Bro Crucefix Past G. Deacon the Chairman of the meeting, did not as in duty bound check or call the speakers to Order, but on the contrary gave them his sanction and countenance". The three named were suspended,

Stevens for three months and Crucefix and Wood for six. All three appealed to Grand Lodge.

Pending the hearing, Crucefix obtained opinions from three members of the Bar separately that notice of appeal suspended the sentence and he therefore continued to attend masonic meetings. This did not pass unnoticed as he learnt when unexpectedly confronted in the Grand Secretary's office on 29th April by the Grand Master. Among the accusations made by the Grand Master as reported in *FQR* (obviously from Crucefix's account) were that Crucefix was "a disgrace to Masonry . . . had led the brethren astray . . . had taken every means to insult the Grand Master . . . by his vile paper [sc. *FQR*] had caused considerable mischief . . . had [while suspended] entered lodges and presided as Master, which was a gross violation of discipline".

The appeals were heard on 3rd June; surprisingly, in view of the earlier confrontation, the duke presided. Wood apologised and was restored to grace; the sentence on Stevens was confirmed. Crucefix was then told his notice of appeal was invalid as it specified no grounds (*FQR* reported "The satisfaction of the Grand Master at this ruling was too apparent to escape notice"). Crucefix was furious and the *FQR* report concluded with a direct attack on the Grand Master to whom he also wrote an impertinent and unjustified personal letter accusing him of violation of the Ancient Charges and stating that having resigned from all his English lodges he "returned into the hands of Your Royal Highness . . . the distinction of a Grand Officer". The duke did nothing about this until a copy appeared in *FQR* when he referred it to the BGP. Crucefix refused to attend the Board when summoned, claiming to be no longer subject to their jurisdiction. The Board recommended his expulsion from the Craft and an Especial Grand Lodge was called for 30th October to consider this. He decided to attend. The throne was occupied by the new Deputy Grand Master, the Marquess of Salisbury who conducted the proceedings with dignity and courtesy. Crucefix delayed proceedings by appearing in Scottish regalia claiming he no longer held any English masonic rank but having eventually been supplied with a Past Grand Deacon's regalia "addressed the Grand Lodge at considerable length, apologising". The apology was accepted by 145 votes to 127.

FQR reported in December that it had "passed into other hands"; but it seems clear that Crucefix remained the guiding force (and financial support) behind it for some time.

In 1838 Crucefix's supporters had begun collecting funds for a testimonial to him in appreciation of his work for Freemasonry in general and the Asylum project in particular. This was presented to him at a meeting of Bank of England Lodge on 24th November 1841; he was able to attend though far from well – indeed, from the time of the expulsion debate his health seems to have deteriorated steadily. Dr Oliver presided at the banquet and made the presentation. The proceedings were resoundingly successful and were of course described in detail in *FQR*. Five months later Oliver was dismissed as DPGM. Crucefix felt he was to blame for this and at once began a campaign for the presentation to Oliver of a testimonial from the Craft. He got himself elected an honorary member of the Lincolnshire Provincial Grand Lodge in order to lead a protest against the dismissal at the annual meeting but harmony was surprisingly restored there, and at dinner he proposed the health of the PrGM, Charles Tennyson D'Eyncourt, who had spoken against him in the expulsion debate but now in reply said Crucefix "had repaid unkindness by charity, and a too hasty judgement by the most benevolent construction of human error"; there could not be more convincing proof of the charismatic nature of Crucefix's personality.

The presentation to Oliver took place on 9th May 1844 in Lincoln. The Duke of Sussex had died on 21st April 1842; his successor as Grand Master, the Earl of Zetland, had a poor opinion of Oliver, who he thought had been too open in his writings about Freemasonry, and no official notice was taken of the event though *FQR* of course carried a full report.

With the duke's death the question of reviving the Christian masonic Orders which, to put it as kindly as possible, he had not exactly encouraged, came again to the fore. Crucefix was heavily involved in this and after much delay and difficulty a new Grand Master for the Knights Templar was installed on 3rd April 1846; Crucefix, though by then he had retired from London for reasons of health, was recalled to act as Director of Ceremonies for the occasion. He thus at last achieved the aim which, no doubt to the annoyance of the duke, he had consistently pressed from the very first numbers of *FQR*, the holding of Great Priory. He had also pressed the case for the Rose Croix, then a degree in the Templar Rite but elsewhere part of the Ancient and Accepted Scottish Rite. He now turned his attention to that.

We have already noted that a patent to form a Supreme Council of that Rite had been granted to Sussex and as there can in general be only one Supreme Council in each country and the duke took virtually no steps under the patent, his death cleared the way for the grant of a fresh patent. This opportunity was not only noted by Crucefix but the Supreme Council for the Northern Jurisdiction, USA, were persuaded to grant a patent to him and Oliver by the threat – probably justified – that a grant by the French Supreme Council, with whom the Northern Jurisdiction had quarrelled, was imminent. It is material for our understanding of him to note that, having been warned expressly by that Jurisdiction not to trust the French, the new Council nevertheless recognised the French at its first meeting, presumably as a sop to those whose efforts he had forestalled. As Oliver later wrote "If any obstacle arose which threatened to defeat his projects, he used his most strenuous efforts to remov

> "The sacrifices [Crucefix] made in a pecuniary point of view towards the attainment of this object [i.e. the Asylum] were so great as seriously to affect his worldly circumstances. He was, however, regardless of this result, and observed to the writer . . . on more than one occasion, 'Never mind the money, I almost think we may live without it'."

Early in 1849 he gave notice of his intention to withdraw from the Craft. Until the very last years his energy seemed unabated but his judgement and prudence were increasingly affected and in such of his private correspondence as has survived there are traces of the strain under which he was working from 1840 onwards. He continued to press the cause of the Asylum, construction of which started in February 1849. It would be formally opened on 1st August 1850, six months after his death.

In the obituary Oliver quotes from letters Crucefix wrote in these last months. They show courage and faith as well as great gratitude for "the affectionate devotion of my wife, her niece and my own nephew". In October 1849, knowing he had not long to live, he moved to Bath, writing to Oliver that he was packing up his papers "to commence the *work of destruction*".

His last letters to Oliver, written as he faced death, throw much light on his character and extracts merit quotation. Thus in early 1849 he wrote: "In Freemasonry . . . have I found more peace and happiness than could have been hoped for; not but that in my course of attaining this partial knowledge I have had to encounter much labour, prejudice and anxiety, but the toil has been abundantly rewarded by the confidence and kindness of fellow labourers in the vineyard." Later he wrote "Some adverse power is at work, and I am too ill to take the helm, or even drive an oar". By July it was "deemed advisable to observe perfect quietude" and to keep his mind from all thoughts of business. In August he visited Hastings and wrote "The merciful Dispenser of all good has vouchsafed me a respite from great personal suffering . . . How grateful I am . . . ".

In September he was briefly back at his Gravesend home but wrote on 22nd "I have only a respite, not a reprieve . . . The cough has returned, though not with all its late violence." He returned finally to Bath in mid-October and died there on 25th February 1850.

To quote Bro John Lane, who wrote the first part of the *FQR* obituary, "his career of trouble, exertion and care is run . . . one perhaps somewhat misunderstood in his objects, and possibly somewhat mistaken in the mode of carrying them out". Oliver, continuing the obituary, summed him up as "Intelligent, active and indefatigable. No difficulty deterred him from the performance of his duty".

What then are we to make of him? Was he swayed by charity or by ambition? Was he acting dispassionately for the benefit of Freemasonry, or for some purpose of his own? Did he aspire to the leadership either of the Craft or of some schismatic Grand Lodge? Is he the charlatan criticised by Jennings and others, the troublemaker of Truman's broadsheet, the jobber and adventurer of Jackson's paper, the ingrate depicted by the Duke of Sussex – or the brother admired by such men as Oliver, Stevens and many others?

On such matters views will be personal. I would not doubt that he had a warm heart and that his charitable efforts genuinely sprang from it. If convinced of the rightness of a cause he would espouse it stubbornly, regarding opposition as something to be overcome even at the cost of trampling on convention, an attitude which must have needled the duke who so far forgot his reputation for calm and fairness as to say in Grand Lodge – if *FQR* is to be believed – that the Asylum project was "nothing but a job, got up by jobbers and penniless speculators for their own selfish purposes" and "Aye, and they talk about establishing another Grand Lodge; I should like to know how they'll constitute it – we've got all the money . . . and a pretty Grand Lodge of beggars, and jobbers, and penniless speculators they'll make of it" – remarks which must reflect what he had been told by Crucefix's critics, by whatever motive they were inspired. The question is how such enmity had been created and whether it was deserved.

The motive for campaigns of character assassination are almost always to be sought in jealousy, envy, fear and similar vices. There is the very rare case where a deeply held belief can cause even the normally fair-minded to feel so bitter against an individual as to try to undermine his reputation but that exception can hardly apply in Crucefix's case because the campaign was both vicious and covert. A motive can however be found in the fears of those who felt their complacency or influence threatened by Crucefix's earliest masonic activities.

When Crucefix founded *FQR* in 1834 he clearly felt that there was much about the government of the Craft that required attention. He concentrated on two specific matters, the enlargement of the two Boards to increase the elected members and the formation of the Masters and Past Masters Club ostensibly to ensure that issues raised at Quarterly Communications were fully understood by those who would be asked to vote on them but were not entitled to attend the briefings given to Grand Officers at the dinners which preceded the meetings. The risk that such a club could form a power base and "pack the house" is obvious but it does not seem to have had that effect. Nevertheless these two proposals would bring new blood into the government of the Craft and help ensure the passage of measures which the entrenched minority might prefer to kill. The easiest counter to such measures would be to discredit the reformer. which is exactly what happened. The duke was jealous of his own reputation as the people's friend and anxious to show that his government of the Craft was democratic; but though perhaps not unwilling to be king Augustus, he was not prepared to be citizen Augustus Frederick and if he could be persuaded by those who relied on him for their positions to see Crucefix as a danger to the concord he had worked so hard to secure, annoyance might overturn his usual courtesy and fairness. This indeed can be seen in his conduct on a number of occasions when he asserted matters as proved about Crucefix supporters which he later had to withdraw, stating he had been misinformed.

If this view be right it disposes of any case against Crucefix as a self-seeking upstart. Whether or no his criticisms were justified is not material. What we have to consider is whether he was actuated by honestly held belief or by an ambition to take control of the Craft. I suggest that there is no evidence of any such intention though it must be admitted that in his determination to achieve what he considered was for the benefit of the Craft he could, to quote Oliver's magnificent understatement indeed be "not very choice in the means he employed" to overcome obstacles. But that seems paltry when compared with the venom with which he was confronted.

We are left then with the picture of an ardent reformer, too intelligent and too impatient for the good of both his followers and himself; a determined fighter in causes if he sincerely believed them good; a charismatic man who attracted great loyalty and a mirror image of great opposition. But a man who attracts no enemies seldom achieves much. He may be labelled ambitious, but the evidence suggests the ambition was for causes rather than for himself. It was perhaps a misfortune for both that he lived in an era of Freemasonry presided over by an autocrat, for however benign that autocrat might be a collision would be inevitable.

Yet had there been no autocrat to restrain him it is at least possible that the plaudits of the multitude and his own abundant self-assurance would make him seek power as the only means to achieve his objectives and it may be doubted whether, having obtained power, he could have exercised it with an even hand. It may be to the advantage of the Craft that he never had that opportunity, but that should not diminish his achievements.

The final verdict however, in my view, rests on another consideration for though he served Freemasonry well, the methods he used provoked a long-lasting official reaction against the very kind of openness about the Craft which he, Oliver and others were trying to bring about; whether or not that was in the best interests of Freemasonry it is beyond the scope of this paper to discuss, but it is a matter on which there is certainly more than one view; and "Time and Life" permitting it would be interesting to consider.

7
The Freemason's Quarterly Review
1834-1840

Introduction

On 1st April 1834, without official approval or announcement the first number of a masonic magazine was published in London: it was put on sale to the public and was called *The Freemason's Quarterly Review* – usually abbreviated as *FQR*. No announcement was made about its ownership but its "onlie begetter", and in fact its founder, editor and financial backer was Bro Robert Thomas Crucefix, 45 years old, a London doctor who specialised in treating nervous and sexual disorders. He had been initiated in the Burlington Lodge No. 113 (London) in 1829, and had served as a Grand Steward (1832). He has ensured that the period of almost seven years during which he edited *FQR* is probably the best documented in the first 250 years of the history of The United Grand Lodge of England. He was also largely responsible for ensuring that it was one of the most interesting, exciting and in some ways disturbing. But the significance of the events of that period for English Freemasonry must be viewed against the social and political background of the time if it is to be fully understood.

Historical background

The Elizabethan era produced a self-confidence and independence of thought and action among the inhabitants of England and Wales which set in motion great social changes; but religious, dynastic and nationalist disputes, often culminating in military action, had allowed the aristocracy to resist pressure for change during the succeeding two centuries. Later the Industrial Revolution transformed what had been basically an agricultural economy. On the one hand, it drew workers into towns where the conditions of squalid poverty in which they often had to work provided a sharp contrast to the equality preached by revolutionaries and evangelical pastors; on the other, it produced a class of men whom industry had made rich but who were politically of little importance because of the limitations of the franchise, though increasingly conscious of the power which their wealth could command. The old aristocracy, for many of whom wealth consisted of heavily mortgaged land, could maintain their privileged position only by coming to terms with the newly wealthy and calling on them to help retrain, by charity, legislation or force the restlessness of the labourers.

In 1832 the great Reform Act began the process of enlarging the franchise which was to continue bit by grudging bit throughout the next hundred years; at the same time a new poor law was enacted, replacing a system of parish relief which had become unworkable with a workhouse regime which provided the unfortunate pauper with a roof but destroyed his identity, divided husband from wife, and gave undesirable powers to overseers compared to whom jailers were often kind and gentle men. It is not improbable that it was the shadow of the workhouse which caused Crucefix to put forward a scheme for building an

"Asylum for Aged and Decayed Freemasons" where such men could end their days in comfort. It has been suggested that the promotion of this was why he founded *FQR* but for reasons which will appear it seems doubtful whether this was in fact the sole or even the primary cause.

The Masonic background

In times of great social upheaval it is easy to understand that a movement which regards all men as equal in its meetings, while carefully preserving the distinctions of rank and religion outside them, may have great appeal. Then as now Freemasons banned discussion of both religion and politics in lodge. It provided a perfect meeting ground for those caught in the uncertainties of social revolution, just as in earlier times it may have provided safety for travellers – which in the author's heretical view is the most likely origin of what has become the non-operative speculative Freemasonry of today.

The newly wealthy who were pressing for recognition in the social and political fields would naturally expect recognition in Freemasonry also. Yet vacancies on the Boards which controlled the Craft were few and, of the dozen or so Grand Officers appointed each year, normally only two of those who might retain Grand Rank after the year would be selected from the great mass of Freemasons. Those whom Crucefix would later call "the elect of the purple", complacently supported the Grand Master, while the brethren who, if they attended, formed the bulk of the membership of the Grand Lodge tamely followed their lead.

Knowledge of Grand Lodge proceedings was not widespread; the minutes of its meetings were often not published for months and then were not informative. A magazine for Freemasons had commenced publication in 1793 but had been of little practical use as a source of information or comment about the Craft. HRH the Duke of Sussex, who had been Grand Master since the Union of 1813 considered that the Craft should exist under a cloak of privacy so deep as to be virtually indistinguishable from secrecy and in 1827 a rule was inserted in the Constitutions that "No Brother shall presume to print or publish or cause to be printed or published, the proceedings of any Lodge, nor any part thereof, or the names of the persons present at such Lodge without the permission of the Grand Master or Provincial Grand Master, under penalty of being expelled from the Order". Reports of such matters nevertheless appeared from time to time in the public press and no official action was taken in respect of them. It is interesting to note that a year after the first number of *FQR* appeared the Deputy Grand Master, Lord Durham, was happy to feel that attitudes were changing: *FQR* quotes him as saying in a speech at a masonic dinner: "Until recently the proceedings at the [Quarterly] Communications [of Grand Lodge] were mere promulgations and registrations of the edicts of the Grand Master, but, Brethren, there has arisen of late a spirit of enquiry worthy of our glorious profession, that has found its way into our legislative assembly, that has brought about discussions upon most important subjects, and this has been happily marked by an especial propriety of conduct, and by the exercise of great intellectual powers. I have sincere pleasure in stating my conviction, that the Grand Master, so far from viewing these proceedings with either distrust or jealousy, is gratified to know that they have taken place". Unhappily events would show that there were definite limits to the Grand Master's toleration and later he declared that he regarded it as his "sacred duty" to enforce the prohibition. To understand these events we must look for a moment at his character.

The Duke of Sussex

The Union of 1813 had freed the Craft from the masonic rivalries of the preceding century. With five royal princes including the Duke of Sussex as members its social respectability was assured – an important matter in those days of social condescension – and for a while all was well even though politically the duke was associated with the reform party and for that reason was unpopular at court, at least until the accession of his niece Victoria in 1837. He had radically changed the course of English Freemasonry by insisting that it must be open to all who believed in a Supreme Being and that christian references be removed from the ritual. But his health was poor; he was prone to attacks of asthma and later suffered from cataracts on both eyes. By 1834 he was becoming blind. Nevertheless, he ruled Grand Lodge firmly while rendering lip-service to its sovereignty. The momentum produced by the Union had slowed dramatically and little had been done for the Royal Arch since the formation of Grand Chapter in 1817.

However benevolent, he was an autocrat and his disagreements with the political establishment and a perennial shortage of cash did not reduce his sense of his own importance. In 1838, when the disputes over the Asylum projects and *FQR* were rapidly coming to a head, he had confidently expected an increase in his allowance from Parliament and had incurred considerable expense in entertaining the Queen at Kensington Palace. The increase did not materialise and the duke, resigning as president of the Royal Society on the grounds that his situation made it necessary for him to leave London, disappeared into the country on a series of lengthy visits to obliging friends. He did not resign as Grand Master though that office required far more in time and energy (though less in expense) than the presidency of the Royal Society.

He naturally shared the pride of the Craft in its charities, the Girls' School and the Boys' Institution. Grand Lodge also administered the Fund of Benevolence for the relief of brethren in financial need, but the rules about relief were strict and inhibiting; *FQR* drew special attention to cases where applications for help had to be deferred because the Master of the Lodge concerned did not appear at the Lodge of Benevolence to support the petition: and petitioners often had to wait weeks or even months for relief which once granted could not be repeated for a year.

The Asylum proposal would not only increase the demands on brethren for charitable giving but would involve the erection of a building and it would be in the Grand Master's mind that in 1834 substantial repairs to the foundations of the Girls' School building had burdened that charity with a debt it could not meet from its own funds. These factors affected his approach to the Asylum proposal and in considering the events of 1834-1840 his blindness in the earlier part of the period and the problems of the Girls' School debt should be kept in mind.

Reasons for publication of *FQR*

Before considering *FQR* itself we should ask why it was published at all. Two obituaries in the volume for 1836 have a bearing on the answer.

The first related to Bro William Meyrick who had been Grand Registrar from the Union; it concluded with this statement: "We acknowledge that to his cautious approbation, warmly yet cautiously expressed, we are indebted for that confidence which has nerved our own exertions; in this tribute of acknowledgment we must however include other senior Brethren of the Order, whom to name in conjunction with their deceased friend would be sufficient honour; but we refrain from motives of prudence."

The second, clearly written by Crucefix, commemorated Bro William Willoughby Prescott, Grand Treasurer since 1826; it read in part: "It is now nearly 40 years since we first remember him . . . 20 years later an accidental circumstance renewed a momentary acquaintance . . . And within these few years we met as Masons . . . the other [Crucefix] was recognised and welcomed. Brother Prescott's mere official appointment would have rendered any approach to him somewhat doubtful upon subjects touching 'the affairs of the Craft'; but there is in the heart of man a secret spring . . . Our course was soon taken – circumstances rendered a movement necessary – the Masters had become inactive, and consequently had imposed upon the executive a fearsome responsibility, which, instead of being rendered easy by division of labour, had become onerous. This situation of affairs, when pointed out to Brother Prescott, first attracted his attention and then rivetted it. Not long afterwards, the writer of this article met Brother Prescott and Brother Meyrick *in council deep*; to their advice he has been much indebted; by their approbation he has been gratefully rewarded."

These two extracts are clear indications that the two most important Grand Officers, the Grand Treasurer and the Grand Registrar (the Grand Secretary had little real power in those days) and at least one other, knew and approved of the project. We do not know who that other or others may have been but Lord Durham is a distinct possibility; a year after publication of *FQR* began, he made the remarks about discussion in Grand Lodge already quoted, and at the Girls' School festival in the same year he went out of his way to comment that (to quote *FQR*) "he could not conclude his observations without acknowledging the great assistance derived by that institution, and by others of a similar nature, from their advocacy by a comparatively new publication that was in every respect a credit to Freemasonry; he meant the *Freemason's Quarterly Review*". It should be noted that a report of a Provincial meeting held at his home, Lambton Castle, was a feature of the first number, and that he was an early supporter and founder trustee of the Asylum project. English masonic history might have been very different had he lived to advise the duke's later years and possibly succeed him but, though appointed Pro Grand Master in 1839, he died in the following year.

Reform

To show that reform was the main motive of the first publication of *FQR*, we must briefly identify what was amiss and what remedies were proposed. Crucefix may well have felt that if successful the magazine could promote the Asylum project but we have no reason to doubt his later statement that he had not intended to bring that matter forward in the early numbers; the obituaries already quoted seem to support this. The failure of administration noted in the Prescott obituary was due in part to complacency in the Boards of General Purposes and Finance but in the main to inefficiency in the office of the two Grand Secretaries. The former was remedied by the addition of four elected Past Masters to each and the latter by a thorough investigation by the reconstituted Boards the result of which was the effective dismissal of one Grand Secretary, Edwards Harper, leaving William Henry White, a survivor if there ever was one, in charge.

We can identify two other objectives which, though originally subsidiary, grew in prominence over the years of Crucefix's editorship of the magazine. These were the Asylum project, which soon became a dominant feature in it, and the future of the Christian masonic Order of the Knights Templar (which at that time controlled the Rose Croix and Ne Plus Ultra in addition to the Malta degree). It would appear that Crucefix even tried to persuade the London Encampments, as what we now call Preceptories were termed, to force a meeting of the Grand Conclave, the governing body of the Order which had not met for 30 years, and *FQR*'s comments about the use of the fees paid for patents in the Order are almost libellous. The duke, though Grand Master of that Order also, was trying to ensure it had a low profile (to put it at the kindest). To sum up, the magazine could clearly be used to support many proposals but it is suggested that Crucefix's basic motives for publishing it were an intuitive feeling that increased openness would be beneficial to English Freemasonry, concern over maladministration of its affairs, a wish to rescue the Craft from what he felt to be a terminal torpor and a desire to infuse fresh blood into its government.

Two years later he would indeed claim that there had been a resurgence in masonic activity in that period, the unspoken implication being that this was due, at least in part, to *FQR*; and in the number for 31st December 1839 he specifically claimed credit on its behalf for a further improvement over the preceding six years. The increase in reports from home and abroad which the magazine was printing by then and official approval accorded to it by the Grand Lodges of Scotland and Ireland give substance to the claim. However, though he was a skilful orator, had considerable charm, and could bind men to him and exact from them willing, loyal and devoted service, his forceful character could and did upset those whose comfort and complacency he had challenged; and in the last two years of his editorship, as relations with the Grand Master became ever more strained and all his work for the Asylum was endangered, anger and frustration came to the fore and a great part of the magazine was then given over to furious comment and self-justification.

Volume One (1834)

We now turn to an examination of the magazine itself. The first number, for April 1834, had 110 pages of which the first 60 only related to purely masonic matters, the remainder containing articles and reports, general news and a detailed Parliamentary Analysis which was dropped later as the masonic content grew. The cover, which did not change, was blue and depicted a zodiac, cloudy canopy, sun, moon, and square and compasses, with the word "LIGHT" below. The size was octavo and the price three shillings. For our purposes the most important part is the "Introductory and General Observations" in the first pages and from which this sentence is culled: "Surely it will not be urged against the conductors of the *Freemason's Quarterly Review*, that its first number is ushered into the world unheralded by the customary announcement of volunteer promises or assurances of high support, and illustrious patronage" – attack was after all the best defence! However, uncertainty about the likely reaction of the masonic hierarchy is apparent from the anonymity promised to contributors. Later, indeed, Crucefix explained that he had not applied, for formal permission to publish because "it *might* have been refused"!

He had apparently had at least one book published previously by Sherwood, Gilbert and Piper of Paternoster Row, London. He now turned to them with *FQR*. An advertisement in the number for December 1836 lists some of the other works they had published and suggests that they were a respectable firm; but the fact that they also dealt in medical publications, some of which were concerned with subjects which were socially unattractive, was later used to vilify him. Firms in Soho, Cambridge, Edinburgh and Dublin were also named on the covers. The printer was William Willcockson of Fetter Lane, London. There was only one advertisement, for the Gray's [sic] Inn Wine Establishment, High Holborn, London, owned by George Henekey and Company; George Henekey was a festival steward in 1834. Later numbers carried several pages of advertisements, many for masonic goods such as Tracing Boards.

Specific items of interest in this first number were: a list of Boards and committees "not given in the Freemasons' Calendar" – the first shot in a war which *FQR* waged against that officially published diary as insufficiently informative for the needs of the Freemason; a celebrated (and unpopular) edict of the Grand Master about entry to the "Glee Room" in which ladies were entertained at Festivals and a letter from the Grand Secretaries, both of which were quoted verbatim. There were also detailed reports of proceedings at an Especial Grand Lodge in Nottingham, as well as those at Lambton Castle which have already been noted; both might have been challenged as contravening the constitutional ban on such reports. Meetings of Knights Templar and Ark Mariners were listed. There was also the first of many anecdotes about men who had escaped death or deprivation at the hands of others on their membership of the Craft becoming known.

One item was captioned "Masonic Intelligence"; the headnote promised "a general summary . . . not only for the purposes of present information, but as a valuable archive of reference for the Craft". It continued: "Such an arrangement has been a desideratum which the Quarterly Communications do not afford . . . Our system will merely be an amplification and illustration of what should, if published in proper time, always precede our own commentary". Since the minutes of Quarterly Communications were almost never published "in proper time" as Crucefix would consider it, this was tantamount to a promise to be the first to publish. Whether these declarations of independence were fully understood as such by the rulers of the Craft is not clear; but no overt step to discourage the publication was taken in those early days, nor would it seem that any whisper of criticism was heard.

The July number began with complementary extracts from press reviews of the first; many were from London papers but the West Country, the most densely populated area outside London, also figured prominently. There was also the report of a speech by the Grand Master which is important for the present purpose because it seems to have been caused by comments in the first number. Appearing unexpectedly at a meeting of the Boys' Institution Committee he launched into an explanation about his attitude to "irregularities" at the concerts in the "Glee Room", protesting that "he was not answerable for the conduct of others who exceeded his directions" (did he mean the Grand Secretaries?). *FQR* commented "His royal highness appeared much moved during his eloquent address, and visibly affected his hearers by the earnest and impressive manner of his delivery".

We also find in this number the first references to the Asylum project and to the possibility of Masters and Past Masters meeting to dine together before Quarterly Communications – the "Masters and Past Masters Dining Club".

Another item was headed "To Correspondents". This was to become a notable feature of future numbers, dealing with queries of every kind, including advice on procedure and status, which strangely does not seem to have aroused any protest from the Grand Secretaries, and comments on the state of the Christian Orders as well as, in later years, cryptic messages about those in authority. It is hard to avoid the suspicion that a number of the questions were "planted".

The October number shows a growing confidence, particularly noticeable in an article entitled "Parthian Glances", one "glance" being about the still troublesome business of the "Glee Room" suggesting that the Grand Master should have checked his information before acting, while a second criticised the year's appointments to Grand Rank, saying "some apprehension is entertained of the difficulty which probably attended the selection – a kindly yielding to the solicitations of private friendship may therefore [i.e. because of the Grand Master's health and particularly his increasing blindness] be more readily excused". There does not seem to have been any reaction to these criticisms.

Development

Until 1839 *FQR*'s coverage of masonic news grew steadily and although some non-masonic items continued to find a place in its pages, it is clear that by then it had become an accepted part of the masonic scene, not only in the British Isles. Dr Oliver, the leading masonic author of the time, had become a regular contributor. Agents for India had been appointed though distribution there was to remain a problem. Crucefix could feel that his venture had been successful even though anticipated profits for the charities had not been achieved.

The duke's sight was restored by an operation in June 1836 and in September *FQR* recorded his "return to the bosom of Grand Lodge on the 7th of this month". On 6th December the matter of the Asylum came before Grand Lodge on a formal resolution to approve the project, moved by Crucefix. Sussex was not present but a letter from him was read urging the Brethren not to approve the motion. Crucefix then spoke at length, skilfully explaining away the Grand Master's fears and secured from a crowded Grand Lodge, to which the Masters and Past Masters Dining Club had no doubt contributed its quota, an approval which the minutes later declared to have been unanimous. That vote being confirmed at the March Communication became an edict of Grand Lodge but the Grand Master did not accept defeat and from this point on, as his relations with the Asylum's supporters and his dislike of *FQR* grew to a point where many felt that the very existence of the Craft was threatened, he seems to have paid attention to Crucefix's detractors

It should be noted that in the *FQR* report of the debate in Grand Lodge Crucefix's speech is given in full yet the Grand Master's letter was merely summarised in an article which described it as "an admonitory letter ... intimating the necessary caution not to be led away by mere feelings, and especially to deal with a protective influence over the existing charities". The report continued "The letter being perfectly unexpected, the mover [Crucefix] was somewhat disconcerted for the moment; – but it was only for a moment; he availed himself of the moral which the letter imparted, and he fairly wound its spirit into his address". In fact, he turned the Grand Master's argument onto its head in a speech of brilliant advocacy. The Grand Lodge minutes reported the letter in full but did not even mention the fact that Crucefix had spoken and simply reported the outcome. The contrasts are obvious and informative.

Much of interest cannot of necessity be included in the space of a talk. Such items are the long leading article in the number for March 1835 and the Valedictory Address in December 1839 which noted the improvements claimed to have been effected through the influence of the magazine. Nor was criticism shirked, as when reports noted "a tedious and uninteresting discussion" in Grand Chapter or "needless discussion" on a report from the Board of General Purposes, or comment was made on lateness in opening Grand Lodge or delays in appointing Provincial Grand Masters to vacancies.

The 1837 and 1838 numbers were the height of Crucefix's achievement as editor. Although 1839 started auspiciously it ended with the Asylum supporters in open conflict with the Grand Master. The 1840 volume, the third number of which was the last edited by Crucefix, was largely given over to detailed reports of disciplinary proceedings against him and others. In these and later reports *FQR* so overstepped the bounds of toleration that in 1841 the Deputy Grand Master, Lord Salisbury, proposed, and Grand Lodge duly carried, a swingeing resolution defining such reports as masonic offences. *FQR* had degenerated from an impartial record into a tool in the hands of Crucefix and his supporters for dealing with what they felt (not without reason) to be the harsh and inconsistent attitude of the Grand Master.

Impact

By 1840 *FQR* had largely achieved the aims of its founder. The administration of the Craft's affairs had become open to the influence of a wider range of members. What may well have been an incipient decay had been halted and reversed. The Asylum project, from which the Royal Masonic Benevolent Institution has developed, had become unstoppable. Christian Freemasonry had been supported against the day when the end of the duke's reign would allow it to be encouraged again. But perhaps the most important result was that the problems of autocratic power in a liberal society had been confronted though it would be many more years before that confrontation would be resolved.

On the other hand, whatever goodwill may have existed in favour of *FQR* among the rulers of the Craft had been forfeited by the violence of its attacks and its exposure of internal politics. Though it had probably damaged the prestige of the Grand Master, he still retained the general support of English Freemasons, who had been forced to look into an abyss of "schism" and had recoiled. More importantly, for better or worse the power of the hierarchy to prohibit any public discussion of the Craft had been greatly strengthened and the possibility of misunderstanding and opposition had sown seeds the fruit of which future generations would reap in sorrow and anguish.

Conclusion

Exciting and disturbing times have their lessons for us. Perhaps the most important to come from the saga of *FQR* is that the Craft ignores social changes at its peril and should, without endangering its essential teaching, consciously adapt to changing times. Another lesson for today from the events we have been considering is that there is a balance between too great a privacy and too great an openness, the disturbance of which can result in danger to the growth, progress and welfare of the Craft as well as being counter-productive in public relations. Where strong emotions are likely to jeopardise reason, great care must be taken to give full explanations and avoid public or even semi-public confrontations if the harmony of the Craft, which is the most precious asset bequeathed to us from the past, is to be preserved for future generations.

8
"Three Degrees and no more"

The Act of Union (1813) between the two Grand Lodges whose disputes had marred Freemasonry in England and Wales during the 18th century effectually excluded all masonic Orders and degrees other than the Craft (including the Holy Royal Arch) from Craft masonry. The Grand Lodge of the "Ancients" had permitted, indeed encouraged, the practice of other degrees by virtue of the Craft warrant and one Order in particular, the Knights Templar, was widespread and popular. The Duke of Sussex had ordered all christian references in the rituals to be removed and there was resentment over this, so much so that a saving for "Orders of Chivalry" was written into the Act.

For 20 years or so matters went smoothly but if there was no overt discouraging of the Templars there was certainly no encouragement from the hierarchy and Grand Conclave was not called to meet. The resentment became part of the turmoil which Crucefix and his supporters caused during the last decade of the duke's life (1834-1843) and was unresolved at his death, shortly after which a Patent for a Supreme Council 33rd Degree of the Ancient and Accepted Rite was granted to Crucefix and the matter of christian masonry again came to the fore. It required only a spark to cause a fire. This talk is about how the fire started and how it was put out.

The title of this talk, "Three Degrees and no more", comes of course from the Preliminary Declaration in the Book of Constitutions of The United Grand Lodge of England. Let us remind ourselves of the exact words of the "Preamble", as it is generally called, printed at the head of those Constitutions today:

> "By the solemn Act of Union between the two Grand Lodges of Free-Masons of England in December 1813, it was [and in the original the remaining words are in quotation marks since they are in fact quoted directly from the Article II of the Act of Union] 'declared and pronounced that pure Ancient Masonry consists of three degrees and no more, viz., those of the Entered Apprentice, the Fellow Craft, and the Master Mason, including the Supreme Order of the Holy Royal Arch'."

That, for a legal document, seems quite clear in intent even though it gives the Royal Arch a somewhat anomalous position. But if we look at the original statement in the Act of Union we find that the quotation is not complete, because Article II in fact goes on to say: "But this article is not intended to prevent any Lodge or Chapter from holding a meeting in any of the Degrees of the Orders of Chivalry, according to the constitutions of the said Orders". Those words quite clearly gave permission to Lodges and Chapters to confer degrees additional to the three Craft degrees which for this purpose include the Holy Royal Arch, and it is at least arguable that this authority was not even limited to lodges existing at the time of the Union for there is no limitation whatever in the text. It clearly meant that a Lodge or Chapter could, by virtue of its warrant, confer any – mark that word – any of the Degrees of the "Orders of Chivalry" subject only to the caveat that this must be acceptable under the constitutions of the Order concerned – not, you will note, to those of The United Grand Lodge. We shall have to consider what were the Orders of Chivalry in due course, but first we should look at the practice before the Union. In doing so we shall have to cover some familiar ground, but to view it in a new light.

You will recall that the two Grand Lodges which came together in 1813 to form The United Grand Lodge of England were the original or Premier Grand Lodge founded in 1717 by four London Lodges and the Grand Lodge of the self-styled Antients founded 34 years later, in 1751. The rivalry between these two was bitter and intense for many years and neither recognised the other as regular, so that even a well-known Brother from one camp might not be able to visit a lodge under the other without being reinitiated, at least until many years later. Mutual recognition did not officially come until the Union.

In the early 18th century Freemasonry almost certainly acknowledged only two degrees and we do not know exactly when the Third Degree began to appear, but early in the century it was becoming quite widely known and it is a hobby-horse of mine to speculate that one reason for the formation of the Premier Grand Lodge may have been a wish to regulate that degree as it grew in popularity. If that was indeed the case, it would surely be unlikely to accept as regular yet another degree, but there was one which was beginning to attract a great deal of support, and that was the Holy Royal Arch. We do not know whence it came, though the avidity with which the Antients adopted it may suggest an Irish origin; all that is certain is that the Premier Grand Lodge, whom the Antients despised as innovators, refused to have anything to do with it, claiming that it was not truly masonic, while the Antients eagerly accepted it, even to the extent of advertising themselves as "The Grand Lodge of the Four Degrees".

At the Union the dilemma was resolved by a compromise; the Royal Arch would be considered to complete the Third Degree but would be separately administered; even so it was not until over three years after the union of the two Grand Lodges that a union was effected in regard to the Royal Arch and the new Grand Chapter was finally recognised by The United Grand Lodge on 3rd September 1817.

The compromise had of course been agreed at the time of the Union; it was the working out of the method of bringing it into effect which took up the time and that delay was very bad for the Royal Arch. However, the first part of Article II of the Act of Union was fully effective from September 1817. But what of the second part? The Premier Grand Lodge had not considered that a Craft lodge could by virtue of its warrant confer any degrees other than those of Entered Apprentice, Fellow Craft and Master Mason excluding the Royal Arch. But this was not the view of the Antients and we must look at their practice to establish what degrees they considered their lodges were entitled to work by virtue of their Craft warrants and then ask the question "Which of those degrees can be said to belong to Orders of Chivalry?" You will note by the way that if a degree was within an Order of Chivalry it was apparently covered by the permission regardless of whether the degree itself had any chivalric content.

It seems that the Antients allowed their lodges to work any degree that might be considered masonic and those were legion; in the middle of the 19th century Doctor Oliver was able to list a thousand or so. Bernard Jones, in his monumental *Freemasons' Guide and Compendium* refers [p 455] to an apron dating from the period 1780-1790 which belonged to a member of an Antients lodge and shows symbols of at least six degrees, all apparently worked by authority of the Craft warrant. In the same paragraph he mentions an Irish lambskin apron of about the same date which has three silk ribbons round the edges, the outer one blue for the Craft, the middle red for the Royal Arch and the inner black for the Knights Templar. Fortunately, we do not have to consider all of Dr Oliver's near thousand degrees because relatively few of them seem to have been worked in Craft lodges here and even fewer belonged to what could be termed "Orders of Chivalry".

Clearly we have to define chivalry and I suggest it implies a connection, however slender or imagined, with the supposed romantic knightly code of the middle ages, and connotes a military flavour. On this basis we can ignore the Mark degree as well as the Noachidae degree of Ark Mariner. The Masonic and Military Order of the Red Cross of Constantine might be thought to be a possible candidate, but as the official history of that Order points out, it is very doubtful if it was extensively practised in 1813. The masonic Knights Templar had however been flourishing long before the Union. An entry in the transactions of a Grand Lodge which operated in the 18th century in York under the title of "The Grand Lodge of ALL England" supports the claim. In June 1780 it listed the "Five Degrees or Orders of Masonry" over which it claimed jurisdiction as "Entered Apprentice, Fellow Craft, Master Mason, Knights Templar, and the Sublime Degree of Royal Arch". That Grand Lodge did not have a long existence, only working from 1725 to 1792; for most of its later years it met only spasmodically, but the Craft in York has a long and respected history and "York Masonry" is still referred to with honour in parts of the world.

If we leave out Bristol, which has a unique masonic tradition of its own, we find that the masonic Templars usually conferred their degrees in Encampments which though they might be held under the authority of a Craft warrant, often met separately from the Craft; but the Knights Templar Order was also a distinct masonic Order in the sense that it had its own governing body (Grand Conclave) headed by a Grand Master and independent of the Craft. It was a Christian Order and in 1813 the Grand Master was the ubiquitous Duke of Sussex who, as is well known, considered that Freemasonry should open its doors to men of every faith which revered a Supreme Being; he had a particular empathy with the Jewish people and under his influence those responsible for co-ordinating the rituals were instructed to see that specifically christian references were deleted.

However, the masonic Knights Templar with its military background and spiritual links with the christian Templars of old, clearly was and would remain christian and was also clearly an "Order of Chivalry" within the meaning of Article II of the Act of Union; but were there others?

My own view is that it was the only Order to which the second part of Article II could apply; but then we have to determine what the degrees were which that Order conferred? It is clear that in addition to the Templar degree itself and the Mediterranean Pass and Malta degrees which are linked to it, the degree or degrees of Rose Croix and Ne Plus Ultra were conferred in the Encampments without any further authority. To appreciate how this fact complicated the issue we must now look at developments outside England and in particular the growth of the Ancient and Accepted Rite of 33 degrees which in many parts of the world regarded the Rose Croix and Ne Plus Ultra as its exclusive property and set particular store by the Rose Croix degree.

The Craft had until the Union been basically christian and the change did not go unlamented; Dr Oliver, for one, was outspoken about it, and his works were as widely read as his words were revered. Craft Lodges continued to hold meetings on the two St Johns' days, which of course are christian festivals, and to regard processions in regalia to the parish church for a sermon as the normal preliminary to any provincial or other great occasion. The duke does not seem to have discouraged this but the fact that he was at the head of a christian masonic Order, the Knights Templar, could have been an embarrassment. He seems to have decided that it must be kept very much in the background, and therefore did not summon Grand Conclave but remained Grand Master with a profile so low that for much of the time he might not have been there at all.

At this point we must look at the myths of Heredom Kilwinning and of the Scottish survival of the Knights Templar. The first asserts that the returning crusaders established masonic lodges in their own countries, and that the Lord Steward of Scotland became Grand Master of a Lodge at Kilwinning there which preserved Freemasonry for future generations; the Stewards were of course the family which became the royal house of Stuart and ruled Scotland from the death of the Bruce to the abdication of James VII and II. The Templar story alleges that at the time of the suppression of the Knights Templar in the 14th century some members of the Order escaped to Scotland where it had not been entirely suppressed and with the help of their Scottish brethren secretly maintained it in exile. It was even claimed that the knights suddenly appeared at a crucial point in the battle of Bannockburn and broke the English array. The masonic Knights Templar emerged in the latter half of the 18th century; it conducted Templar and Malta degrees.

During the 18th century there had been a steadily increasing interest in Freemasonry on the European continent. Masonic myth, or tradition if you prefer to think of it in that way, is insistent in referring to the influence of jacobite refugees as one reason for this and there may be a modicum of truth in that. If indeed jacobite Freemasons sought consolation for the pangs of exile by meeting together in lodges they may well have involved their French hosts in their masonic pursuits and so in the legends. However it happened it is clear that a considerable number of Frenchmen became fascinated by Freemasonry and with typical gallic fervour started to develop it with flair, imagination and a total disregard for historic truth. In this way a totally new, wholly mythical and passionately believed form of masonic history developed which is still trotted out as true by romantics and self–styled historians today. As a result a number of new degrees and, in due and inevitable course, orders, emerged. Many of these seem to have been philosophical, but some were military in nature. Most have sunk into the mud at the bottom of the pond of history, but one Order in particular survived, the Rite of Perfection of 25 degrees which, being extended to 33 degrees in 1786, became the Ancient and Accepted Rite which still flourishes today. Of this Rite the Rose Croix and Ne Plus Ultra degrees, which in England and Wales were part of an "Order of Chivalry", formed part and the myths of the survival of the Templars and of Heredom Kilwinning were so embedded in it that it might well have a claim to be considered an "Order of Chivalry".

The Ancient and Accepted Rite was not officially active in England and Wales during the lifetime of the duke, but he had obtained a patent establishing him as its head here and had used it to set up a Supreme Council, the governing body of the Rite in any territory, though he had done no more. However, the Rose Croix and Ne Plus Ultra degrees which continued to be conferred in the Encampments seem clearly to have been within the exception in the second sentence of Article II. So as these degrees were also found in the Ancient and Accepted Rite, and that Rite might be considered an "Order of Chivalry", what would be its position under Article II? My own view would be that since the Rite as such had not been practised here prior to 1813 it could not come within Article II; but the position could be doubtful and to establish it would be divisive and detrimental to harmony as we shall see.

When the duke died in 1845 the situation became even more confused. The patent for the Ancient and Accepted Rite granted to him had lapsed on his death while the Knights Templar were left under the control of an aged Brother [Burkhardt] whom the duke had appointed – probably illegally – as deputy for life. Dr Crucefix, who in 1834 had founded the *Freemason's Quarterly Review* which the duke considered to breach masonic secrecy, had used that magazine (among other purposes) to campaign for the revival of the Grand Conclave of the Order. Having achieved that after the duke's death, he then secured for himself and Dr Oliver a patent to form a Supreme Council of the Ancient and Accepted Rite for England and Wales. He was thus able to establish the Rite here and this of course included the degrees of Rose Croix and Ne Plus Ultra. After some preliminary skirmishing the Knights Templar in effect abandoned them to the new Supreme Council. This however, could hardly affect their status under the Act of Union and a very complex legal problem could have arisen. When eventually it did arise it was settled in an outlandish way and without challenge by the extraordinary affair of Right Worshipful Brother William Tucker, to give him his Craft rank – Most Illustrious Brother in the Rite.

Tucker was a prominent Dorset man who had become very active in that county in masonic matters. In 1846, he was appointed Provincial Grand Master for Dorset by the new Grand Master the Earl of Zetland. We know that in 1846 Tucker was also Provincial Grand Master of the Dorset Knights Templar – Provincial Prior would be today's term – and he had acquired the Rose Croix degree and presumably Ne Plus Ultra. In December 1846, the year at the beginning of which he had become head of the Craft in Dorset, he was elected to membership of the 33rd degree and to membership of the Supreme Council.

By the end of 1846 therefore he was in positions of authority in Dorset in the Craft, Knights Templar and the Ancient and Accepted Rite and he seems to have held strong views about the place of each in an overall masonic design. He gave startling proof of those views at his craft provincial meeting in 1853 by appearing clothed in his craft clothing as Provincial Grand Master while at the same time wearing some parts of the regalia either of the Knights Templar or the Ancient and Accepted Rite. Further, in his addresses at the meeting he referred specifically to Article II saying "Thus the chivalric Orders are allowed but not recognised; still their existence is fully admitted". He then went on not only to commend the "higher degrees" in general, and the Rose Croix in particular to "all young masons", but while protesting the support of the Supreme Council for the Grand Master he continued "we [that is, the Supreme Council] merely take up Masonry where it has been let drop in England; and endeavour, as far as in us lies, to grant those degrees without which no Mason can be called perfect . . . ". This of course was in direct contradiction to the statement in the Act of Union that "pure ancient Freemasonry" consisted of three degrees and no more, and the only justification for such statements would have to lie in the saving in the second part of Article II, as from his remarks about it he seems to have appreciated.

All this came to the notice of Lord Zetland, who instructed the Grand Secretary to demand an explanation, sensibly basing his enquiry on the ground that Tucker appeared to have breached the craft clothing regulations of 1847, rather than courting a head-on collision over his comments about Article II.

In his reply Tucker took a high-handed attitude as the following extract from his letter shows: "If your Lordship will take the trouble to make the inquiry, it will be shown that the late George IV, and the Duke of Sussex wore non-Masonic jewels with the full Masonic costume of G.M. This combination of non-Masonic with Masonic decorations is by no means uncommon in many Provinces, and not always discountenanced by P.G.Masters [that is, Provincial Grand Masters]. I am aware that it is irregular." In including that last sentence he was perhaps rather less than sensible and certainly courted censure; and though he was correct in asserting that the late king and duke had each worn non-masonic jewels with masonic clothing, and though on at least one occasion the duke had worn masonic jewels on a non-masonic occasion, none of that saved him.

After intense internal debate and under the insistent pressure of the Grand Registrar the Grand Master eventually agreed that Tucker must be dismissed as head of the Craft in Dorset. William White, the aging Grand Secretary who had held office since 1809 was a master of the sardonic phrase and the reply Tucker received was written in his most blasé manner; it informed him that Lord Zetland peremptorily "relieved [you] of the burthen of an office, the duties of which it is manifest you cannot longer discharge without a sacrifice of your convictions". The basis for the action however, was not the expressions Tucker had used in his address but that, to quote the letter again, "out of Lodge everyone may wear whatever decorations he chooses, and express whatever opinions may please him; it is only within the Lodge walls that the laws forbid the introduction of aught which might excite differences of feeling and be a prelude to personal discord and contention". It is clear that whatever the second part of Article II of the Act of Union may have meant in 1813 and although that Act was still the charter of The United Grand Lodge, the Grand Master considered it to be meaningless in 1853. It is perhaps the final irony that in modern times when the RMBI set up a home in the West Country they should have named it after the Grand Master who had so unceremoniously sacked a popular local Provincial Grand Master; but of such ironies is the tapestry of history composed.

There can be little doubt that any overt attempt to modify or abrogate any part of the Act of Union would have met with opposition, and all who have the welfare of the Craft at heart will agree that Lord Zetland was well advised to avoid a "state trial" and simply to cancel Tucker's patent, as he was fully entitled to do, basing the action on a blatant and deliberate breach of clothing regulations. But it is quite obvious that the real reason for that action was the need to demonstrate once and for all to the English Craft that in the eyes of its rulers "Free and Accepted Masonry consists of three degrees and no more", something which it spectacularly achieved.

9

A Masonic Tour of Peterborough Cathedral

This talk originated as a paper read to a non-masonic body. It is included here for three reasons: first, it throws light on the way in which the Craft – in the Provinces if not in London – presented itself to the public in the late 19th and early 20th centuries; second, it shows the close relationship between Freemasons and the Church, particularly the Anglican Church, during that period; and third, it will hopefully be an incentive to those who may be interested to find out more about these relationships in their own areas, for there were many masonic processions and church services in the Provinces over that period.

Much has been written about the history of Peterborough Cathedral and it may seem that little more of general interest can emerge. But both ecclesiastical and social historians, and indeed most other writers ignore one aspect which merits attention, the links between the Cathedral and the Freemasons. For this neglect the Craft must take the blame because of the excessive privacy in which it wrapped itself in the years between the two World Wars, particularly in the 30s, and for over a decade after the second. Prior to that, as we shall see, it had not shunned publicity and on grand occasions a church parade in regalia was not unusual. Many of the clergy of all shades of the christian faith were members. However, by the time that the Craft was ready to return to its older open attitude, theological studies had been influenced by new thinking and new methods. The Craft probably felt itself respectably free of any need to defend its tenets, particularly since those are based on high moral standards and the brotherhood of human beings of every creed or colour; but although "pure" ancient Freemasonry" is only open to men who believe in a Supreme Creator, it does not require that belief to be christian and in the new climate this led to a clash with a vocal section of the churches with what one might describe as a somewhat narrow theological view. As a result, some Christians felt quite sincerely that they were led to take a hostile view of its activities. The shock to the Craft of this attitude has probably been underestimated but one immediate, if temporary result has been a diffidence among some of the clergy about masonic involvement.

The reason for stating all this is not by way of defence of the Craft or attack on the theologians, but because the situation today as perceived by the public is thus very different from that of the Victorian and immediate post-Victorian periods, which are the times with which this talk is chiefly concerned, and the links between Cathedral and Craft can therefore only be understood in the light of the historical context. Personal relationships at both diocesan and cathedral level are in fact friendly here, as in many other dioceses; but Freemasons must realise that there are those who may find any association of the Cathedral with Freemasonry surprising or even reprehensible. Obviously we believe such feelings to be misguided but they exist. Nevertheless, such associations are part of the heritage and the social history of both church and city and should be recorded as such.

The whole building is of course an example of the masons' craft and contains "mason marks", the devices cut into the stones by the operative masons who shaped them though those of which the author has certain knowledge can be appreciated only by those with a stronger head for heights than his; but it is with speculative, not operative, Masonry that this paper is concerned.

With that introduction, let us start our tour, beginning of course at the world-famed West Front. As you enter, there is a small door on your right; an inscription tells you that the former library to which it gives access was restored at the expense of W. T. Mellows MBE, MA, ASA, and his wife in memory of their son. Tony Mellows was serving with the Special Air Service, during the Second World War when he was captured and brutally tortured before being murdered; another memorial to him is in the window in St John's parish church nearby, commemorating the Ruddle family, many of whom were of course Freemasons, including Daniel Ruddle who, in about 1800, made the painted pedestal, now being renovated, for the lodge room at Peterborough.

W. T. Mellows lived in the Precincts at The Vineyard, which is adjacent to the east end of the building (commonly called the New Building because it was only erected in the 15th century). He was a solicitor, being Town Clerk 1919-1930, a post which in those days could be held by a solicitor in private practice. He and his brother Lt. Colonel Arthur Mellows, D.L., were members and past masters of The Fitzwilliam Lodge. He became lodge secretary for a short period in 1942 and was well known as a scholar, spending many hours in the cathedral library studying the old manuscripts, including the Peterborough copy of The Anglo-Saxon Chronicle, preserved there until Dean Wingfield Digby transferred them to the custody of Cambridge University. He was cathedral treasurer and chapter clerk 1936-1946, and archivist 1946-1950. He died in 1950; had he lived a few days longer he would have been the recipient of a Lambeth doctorate. Both he and his brother held provincial rank in this Province.

The fact that the former library is used as the song school reminds us of the close link between the cathedral choir and The King's School and so with Schola Regia Lodge 9105.

Passing through the porch into the spacious beauty of the Norman nave with its clear view to the high altar and its unique painted ceiling, you will see a brass plaque on the first column in the south. It bears two masonic devices, the square and compasses and the two interlaced triangles sometimes known as the seal of Solomon, and commemorates Harry Plowman who was dean's verger for many years prior to his death in February 1900. He was well known and respected in cathedral and masonic circles and for many years was tyler, or outer guard, for St Peter's Lodge; on 12th May 1892 he presented a new kneeling stool to the Lodge, the woodwork of which he stated came from the old-work (sic) of the Cathedral choir, then being rebuilt. This is probably the stool with masonic emblems carved on its sides which is still used in Peterborough lodges today. After his death a meeting was called by the cathedral authorities to consider providing a memorial to him at which Bishop Glyn expressed the wish that the Freemasons would join with the cathedral authorities "instead of acting in the matter themselves" – a wry acknowledgement of the stubborn independence of the Peterborians of those days and which seems to hint at some previous independent action by the brethren of St Peter's Lodge which had displeased the clergy.

Harry Plowman lived at 3 Minster Precincts and on his death was succeeded as dean's verger and as tyler of the lodges by his son, of the same name; we shall meet him again later.

Towards the east of the south aisle is a memorial to another Freemason, John Connor Magee, Lord Bishop from 1868 to 1891, Irish by birth, he was well-known for the resounding oratory and practical content of his sermons. Consecrated Archbishop of York in 1891, he died before he could be instituted. In the masonic library here is the text of a sermon he preached at a service in the Cathedral reportedly attended by more than 5,000 people and held in connection with the meeting in the city of Provincial Grand Lodge on 19th May 1870. On that occasion the Provincial Grand Master, the Duke of Manchester, had been conducted from the Great Northern Hotel just outside the railway station, along Cowgate to the Cathedral by the brethren of the Province in full regalia and "ranged under their respective banners" as the ritual describes it, in a procession led by the band of the 6th Peterborough Volunteer Rifle Corps – a change from earlier occasions when the duke had been escorted by his own private army. The Grand Secretary, Bro John Hervey, a Past Master of St Peter's Lodge was present, no doubt resplendent with the mass of masonic jewels which it was then the fashion to wear, as shown in his portrait a replica of which appeared on the prospectus for the recent cassette and compact disk issue of the history of the Craft. The weather was fine and the route was well lined by spectators. The London and North Western and Great Northern railways had run special trains for the occasion. The L&NWR later tried to get payment out of St Peter's Lodge for use of an engine and the brethren would seem to have been somewhat peeved at the suggestion that they were liable for it.

Six years later on 1st June 1876 the brethren went in procession to the Cathedral "through the College grounds and the dean's garden" – presumably the dean was on the square! – and after a special service paraded to the site where a new aisle for St Mary's church (since demolished) was to be built. Lodge of Antiquity, now No. 2 but the oldest extant masonic lodge in the world and a founder of the Premier Grand Lodge established in 1717, had lent one of its treasures for the occasion, the ancient maul which masonic tradition informs us, probably incorrectly, was handed by Sir Christopher Wren to King Charles II for the king to use in levelling the foundation stone of the new St Paul's Cathedral – which has lasted longer than has the St Mary's building. This maul is still presented by the Master of the Lodge to the Grand Master on certain state occasions. The stone laid on this occasion was accidentally demolished when the church was rebuilt.

Moving on to the east end of the south aisle we come to the memorial to Thomas Deacon, founder of Deacon School with which Thomas Deacon Lodge 9126 is associated. It was in the old school premises, now part of the Queensgate shopping complex, that the Earl of Euston consecrated The Fitzwilliam Lodge in 1895.

The area of the choir next demands attention. When it was rebuilt in 1889 subscriptions were sought for the cost and on 3rd May Dean Perowne wrote in a letter to two former choristers whom he knew to be Freemasons, E. Vergette and H. C. Clarabut: "Several persons have kindly promised to give us one or more Stalls, and I gladly hail the suggestion made by you, two old Chorister boys, that you should endeavour to raise amongst your Masonic brethren a sufficient sum to provide a Stall or Stalls." He concluded "I can assure you we should be much gratified to have the Masons in this way directly and permanently connected with the Cathedral of Peterborough".

The dean's appeal did not pass unheard and enough was raised to provide three stalls, each costing about £300; as there can only have been about 50 active Freemasons in the City at that time, though the nominal membership of the Lodge was about double that figure, this was a noteworthy achievement when £200 was looked on as a fair annual wage. The stalls are numbered XI, XII and XXIV; each bears masonic symbols. Though no definitive record of when and by whom these were put in place has been found, there are some pointers, as we shall see; meanwhile we can consider each stall in turn.

On stall XI there is the well-known device of a square and compasses but within the arms of the compasses there is an irradiated letter "G" – this is a Scottish masonic emblem; square, level, plumb rule and maul, grouped together in a not untypical Scottish manner are also depicted – a sort of masonic *memento mori*. There is also a pentalpha with (of course) the point upright, sometimes known as the shield or star of David or (as with the interlaced triangles) the seal of Solomon; as a christian symbol it has been claimed as representing the five wounds of Christ; to the Pythagorians it was a symbol of health; it is also the Talisman or morning star. It is of course one of the symbols used to denote membership of the Chapter or Royal Arch particularly in Scotland. It was used in medieval times as a doormark to keep out witches and so some amusement was felt when it was included in the design for the floor tiles at the entrance to Freemasons' Hall in Great Queen Street, London, when it was rebuilt in the 1930s.

On stall XII there are three devices. In the centre is a circle with interlaced triangles, as found today in the Royal Arch Chapter. On the left as you look at it is the representation of a keystone, the well-known emblem of Mark Masonry. On the right a pair of compasses are extended within which is a pelican in its piety, the distinctive badge of the 18th, Rose Croix, degree of the Ancient and Accepted Rite. This shows a pelican with its beak thrust into its breast to obtain the blood with which it was said to feed its young, symbolically an emblem of Christ the Redeemer. In most masonic jurisdictions the Ancient and Accepted Rite is universalist, only requiring its member to affirm their belief in a Supreme Being.

It is only in the jurisdictions of the Supreme Councils of England and Wales, Ireland, Scotland and a few others that a man must confirm his acceptance of the trinitarian christian faith before he can become a member of the Rite. The jurisdictions are described here in that way because the three home councils have a goodly number of chapters overseas. The reason for this insistence on a christian belief as a qualification for membership is that two of the principal degrees of the Rite, the 18th or Rose Croix and the 30th or Ne Plus Ultra, were practised here in Knights Templar Encampments (as Preceptories were then called) which antedated the formation of the Rite in 1786 and were of course christian. The patent under which the present Supreme Council for England and Wales was formed was not granted until 1845 and as you can read in the recently published history, *Ancient and Accepted*, it was some time before the Templars could be persuaded to cede control of those two degrees to it. By way of interest, the patent was granted to Dr Crucefix, who reconstituted St Peter's Lodge here, now No. 442, in January 1837 and after whom one of the city's Rose Croix Chapters is named, and Dr George Oliver, "the sage and historian of Masonry" who was initiated in the old St Peter's Lodge, Peterborough in about 1802 and whose Grand Lodge certificate is framed on the wall in the main lodge room while his portrait hangs on the landing outside the second lodge room.

Back to the Cathedral! Stall XXIV also has three devices and these are of special interest. On the right is a representation of the badge or jewel worn by Grand Chaplains and Past Grand Chaplains; it is circular, which would imply an acting rank but in this case that would be wrong, as we shall see. Within the circle is a triangle on which and with an accompanying glory is an open Bible. There have been very few priests in the Province of Northamptonshire and Huntingdonshire who have attained the rank of present or past Grand Chaplain, but we can make a deduction about origins here. The central device is a complete achievement of arms which are those of the Earl of Carnarvon and as we shall see, the 4th Earl was in the Cathedral in 1884 as Pro Grand Master of the Grand Lodge. By way of confirmation, the remaining device, that on the left, is a representation of the jewel worn by the Grand Master and Pro Grand Master, a pair of compasses extended on the segment of a circle and enclosing an eye within a triangle, both irradiated. A glance at the Book of Common Prayer allotted to the stall shows that in May 1890 the Reverend Samuel John Woodhouse Sanders, LL.D. was installed there; masonic records confirm that he was initiated in The Pomfret Lodge No. 360, Northampton, the senior lodge in the Province, in 1876 when he was headmaster of Northampton Grammar School; he was Master of that lodge in 1885. A photograph of members in 1890 shows him as a short man with a full beard. He was appointed Provincial Grand Chaplain in 1879, 1885, 1890 and 1891 and promoted to the Past Rank of Grand Chaplain in The United Grand Lodge of England in 1887. It seems reasonable to assume that, hopefully with the approval of the Pro Grand Master, he persuaded the Dean and Chapter to allow him to place on the stall not only the symbol of his own Grand Rank but also devices which would commemorate a great occasion in the Cathedral's history to which we shall shortly come.

Dean Perowne's letter being dated in 1889, and Sanders' occupation of stall XXIV beginning in the following year suggest that the emblems on stalls XI and XII may also well have been put in place late in the 19th century or early in the 20th. No masonic connection for stall XI has as yet been traced. For stall XII however we have a plethora of candidates, for from 1908 to 1946 it was continuously occupied by Freemasons: Lloyd Timothy Jones of All Saints, Northampton 1908-1920, Arthur Fairclough Maskew of St Paul's Peterborough 1920-1944 and Richard Blakeney 1944-1946. Jones joined The Pomfret Lodge on 2nd November 1897 and was Provincial Grand Chaplain in 1901. Maskew was noted for his forthright behaviour, as when he quietened a noisy demonstration against Lord Burghley in the Church Hall of St Paul's church here or when on another occasion, someone having poisoned his dog, he posted a notice on the church door challenging the poisoner to fight him. Blakeney, who was a staunch conservative, seems to have been noted both for the brougham in which, with top-hatted coachman and whip on the box, he and his wife were often seen in Peterborough and for his friendly but ferocious arguments over politics with Dean Simpson, an equally staunch socialist. The emblems on the stall would suit any of the three. Maskew was Master of The Fitzwilliam Lodge in 1902, Blakeney in 1930; portraits of both are in the recently published centennial history of The Fitzwilliam Lodge.

Moving into the north aisle, we come to the column supporting the north-east of the central tower. The north-east corner is of course the traditional place for laying a foundation stone and so this site was chosen as appropriate for a stone to commemorate the rebuilding of the tower after its near collapse. The inscription on the plate on the upper stone reads:

> This chief corner stone of the North East Pier
> of the central tower was laid by
> The Right Honourable the Earl of Carnarvon
> Pro Grand Master on behalf of
> His Royal Highness Albert Edward Prince of Wales
> M.W. Grand Master in full masonic form
> on Wednesday 7th May 1884.
> J. J. S. Perowne D.D., Dean"

Here we surely have the explanation of Lord Carnarvon's arms and the Pro Grand Master's badge on stall XXIV. The occasion was one of considerable splendour; it had been the intention of the Prince of Wales (later King Edward VII) to perform the ceremony himself, but the court being in mourning for the death of the Duke of Albany, also a Freemason, the Prince could not attend. The duty therefore devolved on Lord Carnarvon as Pro Grand Master. He was a statesman of note. As Secretary of State for the Colonies he had been responsible for the British North America Act of 1867 which established Canada on a federal basis; in 1885, the year following his visit to Peterborough, he became Lord Lieutenant of Ireland, where he had to deal with Parnell and the Irish Home Rule party which was regularly disrupting the business of the London Parliament.

The cathedral ceremonies had been preceded by a meeting of Provincial Grand Lodge, opened at 10 a.m. in the Fitzwilliam Hall, Park Road. In the absence abroad of the Provincial Grand Master, the Duke of Manchester, this duty was performed by his deputy, Bro Butler Wilkins of Northampton. At 11.15 Lord Carnarvon opened an Especial Grand Lodge and a procession of about 800 masons was then formed under the direction of the Grand Director of Ceremonies, Sir Albert W. Woods, Garter King of Arms to escort him to the Cathedral; the Junior Grand Warden, the then Lord Mayor of London, carried the plumb rule, the Senior Grand Warden, Lord Cremorne, the level and Lord Holmesdale, acting as Deputy Grand Master, the square. Freemasons of the Province carried the cornucopia, ewers, trowel, mallet, and the three columns – Ionic, Doric and Corinthian. This lengthy and spectacular procession was led by the band of the Coldstream Guards, and proceeded to the Market Place (now Cathedral Square) whence the Mayor, Alderman Barford, and members of the Corporation led it to the Cathedral where Dr Perowne received them. After a short service the stone was formally tried and declared plumb, square and level. In a cavity in the lower stone various items were deposited in accordance with tradition; these were reportedly placed in a bottle and comprised: a copy of that day's *Times* newspaper, documents signed by the Dean and Chapter, a list of subscribers to the Restoration Fund, and copies of the Grand Lodge programme for the day and of the summonses issued by Provincial Grand Lodge and St Peter's Lodge as well as samples of coins then in current use, sovereign and half sovereign in gold, half crown (2/6d), florin (2/-), shilling and sixpence in silver and a penny, halfpenny and farthing in bronze; it must have been some bottle. When these ceremonies had been completed Bishop Magee gave the blessing, and the singing of the National Anthem led by the Coldstreamers' band closed the proceedings, apart of course from the inevitable banquet which was served "in a monster tent in the field adjoining the hall" – where it would today be hard to find room to pitch an army bell tent.

We now move to the exterior of the building, to the point on the north side where the east wall of the transept joins the main fabric, the traditional site of the Lady Chapel. There a large flying-buttress supports the north wall and inspection will reveal on its face a square and compasses superimposed on a triangle, traditionally the mason's mark of approval, and in Roman numerals the date 1923. There appears to be a further pair of compasses higher up. On the rear of the buttress you will find this inscription:

CONFIRMA HOC DEUS
QUOD OPERATUS ES IN NOBIS

THE FREEWILL OFFERING OF THE FREEMASONS OF
NORTHAMPTONSHIRE AND HUNTINGDONSHIRE
LEICESTERSHIRE AND RUTLAND
CAMBRIDGESHIRE AND OTHER PROVINCES

The story behind this begins on 18th May 1922 when Freemasons from the three Provinces named brought to the Cathedral the money they had collected for building the buttress. Leicestershire was of course within the Diocese of Peterborough until 1926. The proceedings were fully covered in the local press and a complete record of reports and photographs which is in the masonic museum here was carefully assembled by the Peterborough mason who was responsible for establishing and maintaining the library and for starting the museum, Bro Frank Caster, appointed Assistant Grand Standard Bearer in 1920, the first appointment to Grand Rank of a Peterborough Brother since Bro John Hervey, already mentioned, who became Junior Grand Deacon in 1854 and was Grand Secretary 1868-80; there is a rather poor portrait of Bro Caster in the Peterborough masonic museum.

Over 1,000 Freemasons attended the cathedral service; wearing regalia, they went in procession to the Cathedral. Last came the Reverend Canon Gray, Provincial Grand Master for Cambridgeshire, in surplice and mortar board and preceded by Bro Plowman – Plowman junior of course – wearing his masonic regalia with a morning coat and top hat and carrying in his hand his staff as dean's Verger. Fortunately it was a lovely day. £1,045 was raised. Afterwards the dean, Bro Arnold Page, who presumably was not unhappy about the outcome, wrote "It really was a magnificent ceremony worthy of the Masons of today and the Masons who built it [the Cathedral] for the glory of God".

A year later the buttress, designed by Bro Leslie Moore, the cathedral architect, had been built and it was dedicated on 12th June. The dean conducted the service which it was intended should be held in the open near the buttress. However, this time the weather was deceptive; all was well at first but almost at once a torrential storm of rain and thunder blew up; it was described as the worst downpour any present could remember and it bustled everyone into the building in short order for the completion of the service. The cathedral organist on this occasion was Bro H. Coleman.

Strictly, that ends the tour; but one other item should be mentioned. When the cathedral choir was rebuilt in 1882 the old stalls of course became redundant and Dean Argles and the Chapter gave three of the canopies to St Peter's Lodge. In 1917 The United Grand Lodge of England celebrated its bicentenary and the Peterborough Masons decided to mark the occasion by placing two large pillars surmounted by globes in the lodge room, one on each side of the Master's chair, and to place one of the canopies behind it with an appropriate inscription and the shields of the three lodges then working in the city – Peterborough and Counties Lodge had been formed in 1903. This arrangement still exists in the Peterborough lodge room today and a full account of the work, with drawings, is in the masonic museum there; as indeed is a good photograph of the old choir before the rebuilding of 1882. It would seem that the other two canopies disappeared while in store.

There were other services in the Cathedral attended by Freemasons and only those of special interest to the visitor have been mentioned. It is a pity that modern conditions militate against the open recognition of this long and not untypical association between Cathedral and Craft. We can only hope that a more balanced sentiment will soon prevail generally, and that the Craft's present more responsible and open attitude towards the understandable interest of the public in Freemasonry will make it possible to compile a full and unbiased assessment of its role in the social history of this country generally and in that of this and other cathedral cities in particular.

PART THREE
THE ROYAL ARCH

The standing of the Royal Arch in relation to the Craft was only established in 1813 and even then it was several years before the chapters of the "Moderns" and the "Ancients" were formally united. Looking at the early minutes of Grand Chapter and noting such matters as the number of times when that body either could not be opened on time because enough qualified members were not present or had to open without any of the Rulers present, one is left with the impression that no-one really knew what to do about the Order. This neglect at the top became reflected in the private chapters and it was some time before any real attention began to be paid to what Dermott called "the root, heart and marrow of Freemasonry".

There will always be those who will join a new masonic body almost automatically, for whatever reason. One of the motivating factors in this has always been the thought that one might learn more about its history and that possibility was of course latent in the Royal Arch. The legend of the rediscovery of lost secrets became probably the most common explanation given to Master Masons as a reason of why they should join the chapter; but it was never wholly satisfactory for a number of reasons, and the ritual, which had satisfied the brethren in the 18th and early 19th centuries, was seen as the 20th advanced as convoluted, clumsy, difficult to learn and in some ways out-of-date. What was rarely considered was the inner meaning of the Order and why it was necessarily the completion of the Third Degree; perhaps this involved more emotional thinking or deeper contemplation than brethren were prepared to make the effort to achieve. Yet when the need for the thinking of the Royal Arch is understood it is clear that without it the Craft "system" is incomplete; that may not matter when all is well but can result in disillusionment when a prop is needed.

Freemasonry is not a religion; Dr Oliver, with some perspicacity, called it "a handmaid of religion". It can only exist in the context of religion and that requires that it should look to things eternal as well as to everyday life. That is where the Royal Arch comes into its own. The beautiful ceremony of Exaltation is full of symbolism, much of it often unrecognised; the later parts of the ceremony contain much in the way of moral teaching but their appeal is not as obvious and the language is dated. Is there a problem here to which we should seek an answer? If there is and no solution is proposed, can the Royal Arch survive? It is with such points in mind that the talks in this and the succeeding part of this book have been included. They can only suggest ways forward and their intent is to set brethren thinking; they may come to the conclusion that all is indeed well, but mere complaisancy may be to court disaster. At least let us think about what is so often considered unthinkable.

10
The Task of the Royal Arch

This talk originated as an Address to the Supreme Grand Chapter of Italy at a time when Freemasonry was recovering from the suppression it had undergone under the Fascist regime and was an attempt to answer the question of why the Royal Arch is said to be the completion of the Third Degree. The old explanation that it concerned the recovery of lost secrets was never wholly satisfactory and recent developments have made it even less so. Nevertheless, the Chapter does have a very important part to play in the masonic "system of morality" but it is a part which is not immediately obvious.

Introduction: Lodge and Chapter

The status of the Royal Arch in Freemasonry under the English Constitution is peculiar and any talk about it can be confusing unless the position is made clear at the start. Since 1813 it has been defined by the second clause of the Act of Union which brought together the two Grand Lodges then working in London; that clause reads as follows: "It is declared and pronounced, that pure Ancient Masonry consists of three degrees and no more; viz. those of the Entered Apprentice, the Fellow Craft, and the Master Mason, including the Supreme Order of the Holy Royal Arch . . .". However, in the Charter of 1766 which established the predecessor of the governing body of the English Royal Arch it is referred to as "this Most Sublime Degree" and "that most exalted and sacred Degree" and in other similar forms. To add to the confusion, the word "Order" has sometimes been used in reference to the Craft itself though perhaps less now than in earlier days. If we are not to lose ourselves in a sea of semantics we must adopt a firm rule and therefore I shall refer to the craft part of the Third Degree as "the Hiramic Degree" and to its completion in the Chapter as the "Royal Arch".

Regularity

The Royal Arch has not always been regarded by the English Craft as regular, whether as an Order, a degree, or part of a degree. There were many occasions in the early days before the last quarter of the 18th century when it was viewed with ambivalence and even distaste by the older of the two Grand Lodges, the so-called Premier or "Moderns" Grand Lodge. Yet early in that century English Freemasonry had enthusiastically welcomed and cheerfully absorbed the Hiramic Degree; so it may seem strange that the Premier Grand Lodge should have set its face so sternly against accepting another which developed and enlarged upon the thoughts on which that degree was based. We have however, to bear in mind the revolution which the coming of the Hiramic Degree must have achieved. It is my personal view that this revolution and its effect have not been fully appreciated. What it did was to turn Freemasonry into a new path. The old two degree system was little more than a pious acknowledgement of christian morality engrafted onto the Ancient Charges of the operative masons. The new degree transformed this by introducing a metaphysical and truly speculative element into the teachings of Freemasonry. We shall have occasion later to examine the shortcomings of the Hiramic Degree and to see how the questions that it raised but did not answer would shape the course of events, but for the moment let us consider the position as it was in England in 1717 when the first Grand Lodge was founded.

The first Grand Lodge

The Bible was then the background against which all thought was set and there was almost universal belief in its literal truth as history, a circumstance which had led to the acceptance of a chronology which dated the Creation as occurring in 4000 or 4004 BC. This established a finite frame for all history and a belief in an early end to the world, beliefs which remained virtually unchallenged until Charles Darwin shattered them in the middle of the nineteenth century. Intellectual and scientific exploration were advancing in the hothouse atmosphere of London and any educated man would enjoy speculating about philosophy, the laws of nature, the scientific and mechanical discoveries which were being made in such great numbers, and of course politics. Such of them as had been initiated into Freemasonry were not likely to refrain from elaborating the relatively primitive philosophy of the early Craft; the formation of the Premier Grand Lodge in 1717 may suggest some concern lest such activities should endanger the undefined but nevertheless revered ancient landmarks. If that is a valid hypothesis the founders of the new Grand Lodge would not welcome any extension of the system while they were striving to control the most recent innovation. Something of the kind must surely have occurred, even if those concerned did not clearly understand their own motives. But however it came about, the early antipathy of the Premier Grand Lodge towards the Royal Arch was to have results which are still with us today.

"An invention to introduce innovation"

Important as the historical aspect is, if we are to understand the place of the Royal Arch in English Freemasonry we have also to establish why, after being castigated as "a masonic innovation", it has not only survived but has prospered to such an extent that it is officially accepted in the English and many other Constitutions as the necessary completion of the Hiramic Degree; and it is no exaggeration to use the word "castigation" for in 1767 Samuel Spencer, then Grand Secretary of the Premier Grand Lodge, replied to an enquiry about it from a Brother in Frankfurt in these words, "The Royal Arch is a society which we do not recognise and which we hold to be an invention to introduce innovation and to seduce the brethren."

"The Antients"

Of the two Grand Lodges in London, the older was the Premier Grand Lodge, the "Moderns", established in 1717. The other came into existence in about 1751 and derived its nickname of "the Antients" from its claim to follow what it perceived as the true and ancient style of Freemasonry, which it alleged that the Premier Grand Lodge had altered in important respects. The "Antients" were keen supporters of the Royal Arch, regarding it as the fourth degree of Craft Masonry; in fact they called themselves "the Grand Lodge of the Four Degrees" and their Royal Arch Degree was worked in their Lodges by authority of the Lodge warrant. Their propaganda was much more effective than that of their rivals; and "rivals" is not too strong a word. Neither of these Grand Lodges recognised the activities of the other and a man initiated under one would have to be re-initiated before being admitted as a visitor to a Lodge working under the other, though in time the edges became blurred and it seems clear that later and before the two Grand Lodges were united in 1813, there were Freemasons who could claim to belong to both.

"The Excellent Grand and Royal Chapter"

The situation in 1765, 15 years after the "Antients Grand Lodge" came on the scene, was therefore that the Royal Arch was known and practised by one Grand Lodge but officially scorned by the other, a number of whose senior members nevertheless had considerable regard for it. In that year, for reasons which are now lost in the mysteries of time, a number of senior and respected members of the Craft in London began to meet together, apparently with the help of the Caledonian Lodge, now number 134, and by 1765 they had resolved to form what we may term a Moderns' Chapter, clearly considering that the Royal Arch was an essential element in the masonic system. The part played by the Caledonian Lodge is obscure, but it is worth noting that it had been formed under the "Antients" about three years before and then in 1764 changed sides and accepted a Moderns' warrant. As an Antients Lodge it would of course have considered itself entitled to work the Royal Arch ritual; perhaps it was this which had led to its involvement in the scheme. By July the group had agreed what has been called "a self-conferred charter" which established a Royal Arch Chapter, the name of which is not certainly known though it has become known to history by the rather grandiose name of "the Excellent Grand and Royal Chapter". Twelve months later, on 11th June 1766, in the presence of 27 Companions the Grand Master of the Premier Grand Lodge, Lord Blayney, was exalted into the Royal Arch in that Chapter.

Lord Blayney

The saga of strange events now becomes even stranger. Lord Blayney seems to have been considered at once not only as First Principal of the Chapter, but also (and apparently by virtue of his position as Grand Master of the Premier Grand Lodge) as self-styled "head of the Royal Arch". Yet in the following year, as we have seen, his own Grand Secretary was denouncing the Royal Arch as "an innovation [designed] to seduce the brethren". All one can say is that it had indeed seduced his Grand Master!

The charter of Compact

It is virtually certain that the new Chapter had great ambitions for itself from its inception; in fact it was probably intended to do two things; the first would be to legitimise the Royal Arch in the eyes of the "Moderns", and the second to outmanouevre the "Antients" in respect of their claimed monopoly of a fourth degree. Lord Blayney at once set about the preparation of another self-conferred charter which has become known as the Charter of Compact. It established a

Grand Chapter and was drafted with a speed which suggests that its form may have been under consideration for some time and only awaited Blayney's authority as Grand Master to be finally agreed and executed. Among those who signed it were Thomas French and James Heseltine who were successively to follow Spencer as Grand Secretary of the Premier Grand Lodge. The new body was to be known as "The Grand and Royal Chapter of the Royal Arch of Jerusalem".

Forgery

That then is how the first Grand Chapter in the world was established and you will note that none of this had been approved by the Premier Grand Lodge. In fact, if you look at the Charter of Compact in the exhibition at Freemasons' Hall in London, you may well think that it was not executed until the following year, when Lord Blayney's term as Grand Master had ended, for the date reads "1767" and there is a "P" (for "Past") before the words "Grand Master"; but closer inspection will show that the date has been altered and the "P" has been inserted after the document was engrossed. How and by whose order this specious exercise in forgery was accomplished we do not know, but someone was anxious to make it very clear that Blayney's action was not that of the Grand Master of the Premier Grand Lodge. When you remember Samuel Spencer's terse and indignant reply to the enquirer from Frankfurt in 1767 you may feel we have not far to look for the culprit.

Effects of the Charter

Before we leave the historical aspect it will be as well to summarise what then happened up to the time of the union of the two Grand Lodges in 1813 as The United Grand Lodge of England. The Antients for once had been upstaged. They could not start a rival Grand Chapter because they had always proclaimed that the Royal Arch was part of the Craft. They did set up a committee of their Grand Lodge to deal with Royal Arch affairs, but it was a very insignificant and ineffectual body even though they did refer to it on occasion as a Grand Chapter. The Moderns still did not officially countenance the Grand and Royal Chapter, but their disapproval became less and less pronounced as the years went by and they soon accepted it as genuinely masonic, something which they certainly did not do for any of the other degrees and orders which called themselves masonic. In 1774 we find James Heseltine, by now their Grand Secretary, writing to a foreign correspondent "It is true that many of the Fraternity belong to a degree in Masonry that is said to be higher than the other, and is called Royal Arch. I have the honour to belong to this degree ... but it is not acknowledged in Grand Lodge, and all its emblems and jewels are forbidden to be worn there ... You will see that it is part of Masonry, but has no connection with Grand Lodge." It is clear from this that in spite of the refusal of the Premier Grand Lodge to acknowledge the Royal Arch a number of its senior members felt that the Hiramic Degree was incomplete without it, a point we shall return to later.

The Union of 1813

The official attitude of the Premier Grand Lodge had not changed by the time, early in the next century, when negotiations for the union of the two Grand Lodges began. The deep attachment of the "Antients" to the Royal Arch and the official attitude of the "Moderns" to it (in spite of the fact that many "Moderns" had found it to be a necessary part of the masonic system) were to prove stumbling blocks to progress towards union; but a way forward was found by placing the Royal Arch under the control of a Grand Chapter (which satisfied the scruples of the Premier Grand Lodge) while at the same time acknowledging it as the completion of the Third Degree (as the "Antients" insisted it to be). In 1817 the Grand Master of The United Grand Lodge, His Royal Highness the Duke of Sussex, formally united the Grand and Royal Chapter and the "Antients" Grand Chapter Committee to be a Grand Chapter to govern the Royal Arch in the English Constitution. Supreme Grand Chapter, to give it its present title, was thus established and United Grand Lodge agreed to recognise its actions "so long as their arrangements do not interfere with the Regulations of the Grand Lodge, and are in conformity with the Act of Union". The grudging tone of that resolution perhaps indicates that the ambivalence which had persisted for so many years had not entirely disappeared; indeed for some years after the union the Royal Arch seems administratively to have been the Cinderella of Freemasonry. Perhaps no-one had any energy left for the work that should have been done to secure uniformity after union had been achieved in the Craft, for no effective steps were taken until 1834 to consider the Royal Arch ritual and try to standardise it. However, the close relationship between the Hiramic Degree and the Royal Arch as its completion was further emphasised by the requirement that every Royal Arch Chapter should be attached to and take the number of a regular warranted Lodge, though the two meetings were to be held separately.

The Hiramic Degree

This administrative separation of the Hiramic Degree from its completion does emphasise the particular importance of the Royal Arch, the reasons for which we must consider later; but it has also had the effect of creating a psychological barrier to progress from Craft to Royal Arch, making it necessary to convince candidates that they should indeed proceed further even after apparently completing the Craft ceremonies; and it becomes important to find out why it alone achieved such recognition. Of the many other degrees and Orders practised in the latter part of the 18th century and which claimed to be masonic, some have survived, notably those which are now enshrined in the Order of the Knights Templar, the Ancient and Accepted Rite, and the Order of Mark Master Masons; but the fact that the Royal Arch alone became so closely involved with the Craft can only be explained, in my view, if it was seen as actually supplying something which was missing in the Craft system as practised by the Premier Grand Lodge. To identify what it was that was missing, we must ask ourselves three questions: first, what does the Craft set out to teach us; then, where, if at all, does it fall short of achieving its aim; and last, if there is a missing element does the Royal Arch supply it? This enquiry is not just a matter of academic interest; it is vital to the promotion of the Royal Arch, because the type of man we particularly want to attract is unlikely to see it as more than an excuse for another night out unless he perceives it as serving a useful purpose in the scheme of masonic teaching.

"A system of morality"

The primary sources of information about the purpose and tenets of English Craft Freemasonry are of course the ritual and the lectures, of which the Emulation working is that which is most widely known and probably most closely associated with the revisions which took place at the time of the Union. In common with most other English rituals it defines Freemasonry as "a system of morality". This makes two things clear; first, that it is concerned with morality and is not a religion or religious sect, and second, that it claims to be a system and as such must be taken to teach a comprehensive code. But what does that code involve? The ritual specifies three ingredients, "brotherly love, relief and truth". Let us look briefly at each of these.

Brotherly love

Brotherly love we can explain as the duty to love your neighbour, whether or not he is a Freemason; for Christians this is of course the second great commandment as proclaimed by Christ who told the parable of the Good Samaritan to illustrate it. It is worth reminding ourselves that the hero of that story was a believer not in the Jewish faith but in one that denied the doctrine of resurrection; the orthodox Jews in fact "passed by on the other side". Yet it was a Jew who told the parable, and he told it to a Jew.

Relief

"Relief" is usually paraphrased as charity; but to us as Freemasons it means much more than the giving of alms, important though that aspect is. It involves, in the words of the Charge after Initiation, "rendering [to our neighbour] . . . every kind office which justice or mercy may require, by relieving his necessities and comforting his afflictions, and by doing to him as in similar cases you would wish he would do to you". It also involves tolerance towards another's beliefs even where those differ from one's own.

Truth

So far, so good; but now we come to Truth and this is much more difficult to define. Francis Bacon in a famous essay wrote " 'What is truth?' said jesting Pilate and would not stay for an answer". I think that question was asked in despair by a man who knew that there are as many different answers as there are inhabitants of the planet; truth will always be subjective for mortal men. Furthermore, the word is used of two quite different concepts; it can mean the reverse of falsehood or it can refer to the eternal verities, the very riddle of the universe and of our being. How does the teaching of the Craft deal with these concepts? The answer, it seems to me, is that it deals with the first but fails altogether to tackle the second; in other words, it provides guide lines for our conduct towards our fellow mortals but fails to place these guide lines in the perspective of eternity. This becomes particularly clear if we consider the Hiramic Degree which was so eagerly adopted by the English Freemasons of the early 18th century. The legend of that degree cannot be considered as a resurrection drama, for that would be to trespass on the preserve of religion which by definition we do not do. It is a story of treachery and dishonour meeting their just reward and of the vindication of the honourable man who kept his oath, who was murdered because he would not break it, and whose body was recovered from an unmarked grave to be reinterred in a manner which acknowledged his worth. After the re-enactment of the murder and the raising of the candidate there is a mention of "that bright Morning Star, whose rising brings peace and salvation to the faithful and obedient of the human race" but otherwise there is no reference that can be considered as in any way spiritual. Surely that unexplained phrase itself suggests that there must be something more. The ritual tells us that the object of the degree is to teach us how to die and "to feel that to the just and virtuous man, death has no terrors equal to the stain of falsehood and dishonour". It is as if the ritual itself was now proclaiming its own inadequacy. Where are the links with eternity and with the teachings of religion which surely we would expect in so serious and solemn a deliberation?

The perspectives of eternity

This, I suggest, is where the claim to be "a system of morality" falls short. It is a matter of perspective; the teaching of which the Hiramic Degree is the culmination insists that Freemasons must believe in a Supreme Being but expresses its doctrines in terms of our mortality and of our duties to our fellow mortals. In this it seems to have veered away from the doctrines inculcated in the Ancient Charges of the Operatives, something which would not be surprising in the context of the political and philosophical attitudes of the 18th century with their emphasis on the rights of man and "natural" philosophy; later it would be emphasised further by the removal of explicitly christian references from the ritual at the behest of the Duke of Sussex at the time of the Union. The element of the eternal is consequently suppressed. Yet the whole philosophy of the Craft, the very meaning of its ritual and teaching, presupposes the existence of the purposes of an omnipotent Creator. For these reasons it does not seem to me that the Craft can claim to have dealt fully or satisfactorily in its ritual with one of of the "system of morality" it claims to teach. Viewed in that light, the emergence of something such as the Royal Arch, which restored the perspectives of eternity to the system, was an inevitable condition for survival in the atmosphere of the late 17th and early 18th centuries with its Bible-oriented philosophy, eager questing for knowledge, and delight in philosophical speculation.

"The root, heart and marrow of Freemasonry"

So we come to the present time and the lessons to be learnt. History has saddled us with a Royal Arch artificially divorced from the Hiramic Degree whose teaching it completes and to which we may feel it rightly belongs. To enter the Chapter a Brother has therefore to make a conscious decision to take up new responsibilities. He may fairly ask why he should do so. The old answer, that he will learn the true secrets which were lost at Hiram's death, cannot be regarded as satisfactory; certainly it does not explain why Lawrence Dermott, the second Grand Secretary of the "Antients", called the Royal Arch "the root, heart and marrow of Freemasonry". But does this still apply? The world has changed since Dermott's day and now we are continually being reminded that its values seem to be those of the materialist. In such a world is there a need for a moral code deeper than that taught by the Craft? For some, perhaps not; for them the Hiramic Degree will be sufficient. But a man who truly believes he is accountable to a Supreme Being will feel the need for a more intimate link with the teaching of his religion. This is the need which the Royal Arch addresses in the companionship of the Chapter by seeking to put the moral teaching of the Craft into the frame of eternity, and when Companions understand and appreciate this purpose of the Royal Arch, the companionship of the Chapter becomes a very real thing. Brethren become anxious to join it instead of having to be coaxed into it, and when exalted they are content to stay as members even though they have to wait to go into office. But we must bear in mind that Brethren should never be received into the Chapter unless and until they are ready for its teaching.

Work in Chapter

So much for what one might call the recruiting side of the Royal Arch. In the Chapter itself we have to ensure that every Companion, however junior, is as fully involved as possible. No Companion can become a Principal until he has been installed as Master of a Craft Lodge; and even the shortened and much improved forms of the Lectures recently adopted in the English Constitution can seem long if care is not taken over their presentation. But when there is a regular sharing of the work, and particularly when the catechetical mode of working the lectures is used, these obstacles are soon overcome.

Finally

I have one more thing to say to you. It has nothing to do with history or ritual, yet it is probably the most important point I have to make, as well as being, you will be relieved to hear, the shortest. No Lodge or Chapter achieves its full potential unless its members enjoy their Masonry; only in such an atmosphere of "being happy and communicating happiness" will the lessons of our system be learnt and others be attracted into the Craft. Solemnity does not preclude happiness, and must never be allowed to kill or damage it. So my final wish for you all is that you may enjoy your Masonry, and in particular, that you may have many years in which to enjoy its happy companionship.

11
The Royal Arch – The Present and the Prospect

The Royal Arch does not deserve to be the Cinderella of Freemasonry but that is what it may be in danger of becoming. It should be accepted as being what Laurence Dermott described it as many years ago, "the root, heart and marrow of Freemasonry". The object of this paper is to suggest what may have gone wrong and what we might do to put it right. Of necessity this must be a personal view, though it does come from one who is genuinely concerned for the future of the Order and its status in Freemasonry. Hopefully the suggestions will be accepted as constructive and will not seem opinionated, pedantic or conceited.

Freemasonry is the code name for a system of morality founded on two basic principles: a belief in a Creator God, and the virtues of brotherly love, relief and truth, virtues which include tolerance for the beliefs of others. These two principles are the basis of the moral teaching of the great religions and social codes but they are most conveniently summed up in that of Christianity, which describes them as love of God and love of one's neighbour. So we start our analysis from that.

In the booklet *Why Join the Royal Arch?* the author has stated his belief that the Craft degrees, excellent as they are in guiding us in the principles of brotherly love and relief, are inadequate when it comes to truth because they concentrate essentially on rules of social behaviour – in other words, on our mortal life, – but do not lead us to think in wider terms. After all, this life is only a small part even of the space-time context, yet the Craft leaves it to the Royal Arch to set the picture in a frame of eternity. If you want to examine that more closely I suggest you read the booklet – the profits go to help masonic charity and masonic education, so you will be furthering a good cause if nothing else.

On the basis of such thinking, the Royal Arch can indeed be the "root, heart and marrow of Freemasonry". But while that may answer the question of why a Master Mason should seek Exaltation, it deals with only one of the basic principles, that of truth; and it is in that sense subjective, even introspective. How does it fit in with the other two basic principles, brotherly love and relief? What does it require us to do about them? And why do only about a third of Master Masons join it, and of that third why do so many not persevere? Here we desert principle for practice.

Let us think about that last question: why do men "drop out" either by resigning from the Chapter or by failing to advance or perhaps just by not attending? I suggest that there are three basic reasons, two of which are understandable. These last are the ritual side of the work and the lack of a sense of purpose, a feeling of "so what?" The third reason is something which has nothing to do with the principles of the Royal Arch but only with the running of the

Chapter: a feeling that it is stuffy, outdated and sometimes, regrettably, dominated by what are deemed, however unjustly, to be cranky disciplinarians. This third reason is not addressed in this paper but it is something a Chapter should think about very seriously if numbers begin to drop.

So what about the ritual? The first part of the Exaltation ceremony is dramatic and exciting – if it is properly presented. The remainder is a preceptor's delight but a nightmare for the slow learner, who may yet be a worthy member. We cannot change the ritual to suit ourselves and any change is always difficult and divisive. We have to realise that the Chapter ritual is not easy to absorb and for those who find such learning difficult it is intimidating. The author of this paper is whole-heartedly in favour of considering and where appropriate varying the presentation of the ceremony, something which is quite different from altering the ritual wording and something which on occasion it would be wrong not to do, as for instance if you have a blind candidate or one with artificial limbs or partial paralysis, all of which he has had to cope with. It would be quite contrary to our principle of brotherly love not to adapt the ceremony to the needs of the candidate. But apart from such special cases what can we do?

First, we must see the ritual in perspective and show more sympathy with those who genuinely find it difficult; however much the thought may scandalise some of you, ritual is only one part of Freemasonry, albeit an important part, and we have all known men who are good Masons and perhaps do a wonderful job, for instance as almoners, but who will refuse to go into the chair because they feel unable to deliver the ritual to the high standard they demand of themselves. Ritual is a means to an end and not an end in itself, not even *the* means. Its purpose is to see that masonic principles, tenets and customs are presented to the candidate in an orderly and understandable way. If a man is sincere in his attachment to the principles of the Royal Arch and anxious to help in carrying its tenets into practice he should in my view be encouraged to take office, and if he cannot manage all the work, well, what about all those Past Principals who would love to get back on the floor?

Even those who learn more easily should not be pressed to do too much or be encouraged to take on work too readily. What is important is that the ceremony should be meaningful, even surprising, to the candidate. He must be both fascinated and rendered curious. Exaltation is quite the most important part of his chapter career and on its presentation will probably depend whether or not he becomes fully involved in the Royal Arch, whether in fact he will think it worth while to continue. A balance has to be achieved between attracting the candidate and preserving the interest of the members and it is a shame that impressing the members, particularly senior members and visiting dignitaries, is all too often given the preference.

Consider for a moment the ceremony itself and ask yourself what was most meaningful to you on that evening when you came into Chapter. Experience tells us that it was almost certainly the drama of the story told by the Sojourners. But if the ceremony is properly performed and the candidate is encouraged to think about it, the lasting pictorial memory will be that moment when the hoodwink was removed. In that moment he saw a picture which he will not forget, but he is not often encouraged to consider its appeal. He is looking at an allegory of the pattern of a Freemason's life. Immediately in front of him are the stones he has had to remove as he will have from time to overcome obstacles if he is to progress in life. Then the chequered floorcloth, which represents the mixture of joy and sorrow we encounter in our earthly pilgrimage, guides his eye to the pedestal which is in the form of an altar of incense, an ancient symbol of worship; the top is covered, emblematic of knowledge yet to be won. He may become aware of the figures lining the path: the companions who will support him on his journey. All this leads his eye to the group in the east and the triangle of sceptres, that of earthly power and duty suspended from those of prophesy and worship and hinting at the omnipotent Power Who rules over all. If he is encouraged to think about this, he will remember it each time he sees an Exaltation and be reminded of his duty to the newcomer and his obligations to the Chapter.

In the second part of the ceremony the author is a firm supporter of the catechistical method of giving the first two lectures; and we should not shrink from dividing the answering of the questions between a number of Companions; so long as order, coherence and dignity are maintained, the more the better: a change of voice is not always, or even usually, a distraction – that is an old wives' tale; such a change can prevent boredom or loss of interest, for each of us can too easily overrate his ability to hold the attention of an audience. So too there is much to commend the practice by which all those who are to take part in a lecture or other presentation stand in the west throughout the whole, but you should be encouraged to experiment and see what works best for you. However, the Mystical Lecture is special and it is doubtful whether it or the Chapter gain from the catechistical method; nor can it readily be divided into more than two parts. As Grand Superintendent the author insisted – and his successor has continued the practice – that in the second part, when a Past First Principal does the work, he should hold the First Principal's sceptre, because the candidate has just made a solemn promise about pronouncing the sacred name "except when acting as First Principal"; but the sceptre should never, never, never be used as a pointer: if one is needed it can be brandished in the other hand. But this is a matter where the wishes of your Grand Superintendent must be paramount and you should only act in it in accordance with his views.

There is another point about the lectures which you might feel is worth thinking about. It relates to holding the interest of the candidate and keeping a sense of intimacy. When the signs are explained, it often happens that the Companion giving the explanation is in the east but the candidate is in the west; between them are the banners and the paraphernalia of the floorcloth. So not only is a great gulf fixed between them which has to be bridged vocally and visually but all sense of intimacy and connection is lost. Again, it is for your Grand Superintendent to rule on the matter but there is much to be said for varying the presentation so that instead of saying ". . . you, my newly exalted companion, will rise and copy me" something is said like "the Assistant Sojourner will conduct you to the east so that you may see and copy me".

Now putting forward suggestions which involve changing the way things are done has probably upset some of you. Remember that the ritual has changed from time to time and there are in any case several different versions; it cannot therefore be an antient landmark and the point to consider is what is right for your Chapter and not for you personally. Of course, these are only suggestions – but they are made because there is something wrong – the figures show that, and where, without altering the impact of the ritual, we can make the presentation more personal and more obviously relevant, there must at least be a case for consideration. Freemasonry is a social phenomenon and like all such phenomena it has had to change to remain the same – adapting to changes in emphasis and what is seen as relevant to the changing social climate. Indeed, it must continue to do so if it is to survive; the trick is to change without seeming to, and to do it cautiously without doing it too late. The present trend is against the verbal pomposity and obscure language of an earlier age, to both of which characteristics the ritual we have inherited in the Royal Arch is prone and we do well to realise that it therefore needs special care in delivery; in particular, it should never be hurried.

We have been looking at what one might term the domestic side of the matter; but there is of course another side; what is our duty to the Craft as Royal Arch Companions? We consider that as such we are a species of elite; but the greater the prestige, the greater is the duty. We announce our standing by wearing the jewel; let us remind ourselves here of the motto it bears, *si talia jungere possis, sit tibi scire satis.* A fair, though free, translation would be "If you could link all these things together to make a pattern, you would understand" – a rather mystical and mystifying statement which appears to mean that a knowledge of the qualities listed in the inscriptions on the jewel will be enough to enable you to live a creditable life here and be prepared for the hereafter. But the most important thing about the jewel in our present context is that it is worn in lodge and so not only invites questions but labels us as a special category of Masons. Our conduct should be such that the Royal Arch jewel will always be recognised for two characteristics: as a sign of experience and as an offer of help.

This leads us on to consider something which is in part responsible for the fact that the full potential of the Royal Arch is not being realised. We must train ourselves so that we can answer questions from Master Masons about the Royal Arch: such questions as "What is the Royal Arch for? What is special about it? Why should I devote more evenings to it when I don't have much time to spare as it is?" Have we in fact thought about answering such quite legitimate and reasonable enquiries? It sometimes seems as though we do not all have a definite sense of vocation and purpose as Royal Arch companions; if so, we ought to think hard about this. One suggestion for improving the image of the Order would be that every companion should be urged to show himself willing and able because he is a Royal Arch mason to undertake any of the many tasks that make for the smooth running and harmony of his lodge. You will note those words "willing and able"; however keen you may be to help, your efforts will be less than fruitful if you have not "done your homework" as the saying is; ability involves knowledge and knowledge involves work. For instance, if you undertook to go out of lodge with a junior Brother while a ceremony was worked which he was not yet entitled to attend, would you be able to answer his likely questions? If a Brother asked you to explain the Royal Arch to him, would you have an answer ready? What do you know about the history of the Order or even that of your own lodge? Never be afraid to ask for help; senior brethren will often be able to suggest where answers may be found even if they cannot advise you directly. If we are to aspire to be among the most useful members of the Lodge, we must equip ourselves for the job; after all, serious thinking is unlikely to damage your health and research does not carry a government health warning. If we are to make our brethren conscious of the existence of the Royal Arch, we must ensure that we, as Companions, have a reasonably prominent profile. There must of course be no question of officiously pushing ourselves forward; but we ought to aim at a situation where, when something has to be done, brethren will look first to the Chapter members to carry it through.

Here we can consider one small suggestion about how the Chapter might be gracefully and modestly supported in lodge. When a task is to be performed which a Royal Arch companion has agreed to undertake, why should not the Worshipful Master – who hopefully will have been exalted – say something like "I should like a member of the Chapter to retire with Brother X and as Brother AB has kindly offered to help in this I ask him to do so".

Hopefully you will agree that so far we have been sticking to practicalities. Now we must go further. We have a problem, one which has already been mentioned in general terms. It concerns the ethos of the Order and will involve an excursion into the theoretical sphere. It can best be posed in the form of questions: Is Freemasonry in general, and the Royal Arch in particular, really relevant to the world into which we are moving at an alarming rate? What need can we hope to fulfil that television, cyberspace, the internet and all the rest of the paraphernalia with which modern progress is bombarding us do not satisfy? Armchair shopping, armchair entertainment, armchair education – why bother to get togged up in dark suits and black ties and try to find a parking place for the car so as to attend Lodge or Chapter? Why desert the family for what may seem a selfish and not particularly cheap evening? Unless there is some point in it, why do it at all?

We do indeed have something to offer society and Freemasonry will continue to satisfy a need, provided we get our house in order. For some, ritual, ceremony and order will provide a personal satisfaction not to be found elsewhere; for others curiosity may be the attraction. But in all these cases the interest will only last as long as the magic holds. However, the probability is that the one essential attraction will be the attitude to their Freemasonry of those who are already members, and that, Companions, means an end to the cloak of secrecy about membership. This cloak is a modern reversion to an old fetish, since for many years and until quite recent times, every Lodge had to deliver to the Clerk of the Peace every year a full list of its membership. This is not intended to suggest that we should go about proselitising, that is, drumming up recruits, nor that anyone should do anything which might prejudice his job; but there must be greater openness if men are to be attracted to join us. One of the reasons why the author of this paper wanted to join the Craft after the war was because he found that many of those whom he thought of as trying to live their lives in accordance with standards of honesty and (to use an outmoded but still expressive word) decency, were in fact "on the square". He had quite a problem trying to find out how to ask about becoming a member. No-one was sufficiently forthright to ask if he would be interested and having moved to a new part of the country it was some time before he could make an approach himself. Another example is that of a man who was a member of a cathedral choir; he became aware of the fact that almost all the other men choristers were Freemasons but thought it was wrong to push in unless he was wanted. One day he found a note in his prayer book, "We can't ask you; you must ask us". Fortunately the modern relaxation of the rule on this – that you may invite a man once, and remind him once – has removed that problem; but we still have to be able to spot the man who may enjoy Freemasonry, be a credit to the brotherhood and benefit from its teaching, and to take the first step in explaining it to him.

There was and is no need for secrecy of the sort we saw in the past; we have nothing of which to be ashamed and much of which we can be proud and we should take full advantage of that recent ruling which, within limits, allows us to suggest to suitable candidates that they might find Freemasonry enjoyable and constructive.

But back to the future! Ask yourself now how you would explain to a friend why he might consider joining us. What benefit would he get in return for leaving wife and kids in order to attend lodge? Material benefit is of course ruled out. How is he going to explain to his family that he is joining something from which they will be excluded? We have moved away from the accepted doctrines of the earlier days of male dominated society and we have to think about these things.

Following on from this, how, later, would you explain to your friend, now your brother, why he should join the Royal Arch? Will he feel surfeited with ceremonies and see no point in more? Has the ethos of the Order penetrated to his understanding or will he think of the whole business as mumbo-jumbo conducted for the benefit of a number of overdeveloped egos? He may well have heard discussions by this time about where the next candidate is to come from, and wonder if that was in fact the reason for suggestions that he should join the Chapter. As an aside, do you see how dangerous the doctrine that "we must have a candidate for the next meeting" is, how self-defeating and detrimental? Once again we come to the importance of each one of us working out for himself why he is a Mason and, in our own case here, why he is a member of the Royal Arch, and what is the relevance of it all to the world of today and perhaps even more importantly, to that of tomorrow.

All this has deliberately been put in stark terms, because it is important not to deceive ourselves. There is a great deal which Freemasonry can contribute to the future and the most important factor in the equation has been left to the last; indeed, it is so important that no lodge, let alone a chapter, will survive without it. On the other hand, where it is present, the Royal Arch Chapter will provide a vital and important contribution for everyone. In one word, that factor is enjoyment. The happy lodge and the happy chapter will survive, perhaps as an oasis of humanity in a robotic world. But to achieve that happiness several things are necessary, of which a conviction of the constructive value of what we are trying to achieve is one of the most important. In addition, meetings must be enjoyable, involve active effort by everyone to preserve harmony and, perhaps most essential of all, tolerant good humour and a real readiness to try to understand problems must prevail. As we progress through the offices and finally through the Royal Arch chairs, the effort of learning the ritual and ceremonial has to be tackled and those responsible for overseeing this must show tolerance and understanding, be as ready to listen as to propound, things which are especially important for that much maligned officer, the Preceptor about whom I once wrote a verse which some of you may have seen:

Are Preceptors human?
We know they wish us well,
So perhaps they really must be –
But its very hard to tell.

Once through the chairs in the Royal Arch a companion too often finds himself "left on the shelf". Past Principals must be made to feel welcome and given opportunities to be useful, not necessarily just in doing ritual; they might for instance be asked to take over a ceremony to help a worthy Brother who is not good at ritual, or to give ten minute talks (very strictly timed!) about the Chapter or prominent members in the past. And why should not a Past Principal be allotted to each candidate on an individual basis as his mentor to advise, explain, help with learning as the "new boy" is invited to do some work, as he should be at an early stage? It is essential, if the Chapter is to be and remain a happy gathering that the newly exalted companions are brought fully into its fellowship. Freemasonry is to be enjoyed and it is worth repeating over and over again that no Lodge, Chapter or other masonic group will prosper unless it is a happy gathering. "Enjoy your Masonry" might well be written over the lintel of every lodge room. It requires great effort and thought on the part of all who are responsible from time to time for the government of the Chapter to achieve such a result, but the effort will be well repaid; it also requires commitment and serious thought about our purpose, and – dare it be said – about our history, so that we can explain why things are as they are and why we are proud to be Freemasons; and let it be emphasised once again that as Royal Arch Masons we must be the committed core of our lodges, but without seeming in any way to become a cabal or to do other than work with and under the regular officers.

So we end where we began, with brotherly love, relief and truth; for in the end it is only with the outgoing attitude implied in those qualities that enjoyment will be achieved and the purpose of our order accomplished – indeed without it there must be a serious doubt whether even the Craft, let alone the Royal Arch, will survive. Enjoyment will always be attractive and enjoyment in the company of others will always have a human appeal – perhaps especially in a world dominated by computers; and coupled with commitment and a sense of purpose it will in the long run ensure that we attract, meet the needs of and keep the type of men we want to join us, and that with their help and our own endeavours Freemasonry continues to perform a useful role for the benefit of society.

12
Is the Royal Arch "A Step too far"?
An address to a Chapter of First Principals

This talk is not concerned with research or indeed with the present but with the future, which includes asking ourselves whether there is a future. It is intended to start you thinking and even questioning some of our present ideas about the Royal Arch, but as that is essentially a part of Craft Freemasonry we cannot consider it in isolation; we shall therefore have to think about how the Craft may develop in the 21st century and indeed whether Freemasonry as we know it can survive the challenge of the future. This in turn means taking account of matters outside Freemasonry, so there is a wide field of enquiry facing us and you will be relieved to know that we cannot possibly cover it fully in one session. Hopefully you will find that you cannot accept some of the ideas put forward, because then it may start a debate while there is still time and dispose of any suggestion that there is no need to bother about the future of Freemasonry because it will continue for ever. So in an odd sort of way, the more you disagree the better will the paper have accomplished what it set out to do.

So, how should we proceed? Well, first we must ask ourselves what we regard as the essential role of Freemasonry in our lives: in other words, why are we Freemasons and why do we try to bring others into our fraternity? This will involve establishing what part Freemasonry fills in the life of the community and whether it will be as it were surplus to requirements in the 21st century. Then we have to consider the place of the Royal Arch in Freemasonry in relation to our findings on all these points; for instance, should it now be abandoned as the essential completion of the Third Degree? Is it in fact as the title of this talk suggests, a degree too far? Should it be reabsorbed into the Craft as it once was under the Grand Lodge of the Antients? All this involves considering how the social mores of the next century are likely to develop and there is plenty of room for argument over that. What is essential is that we should be honest with ourselves.

For a start, do we bring our friends into the Craft because of its high moral standards, or because we enjoy the social side and think that they would too? Or are we simply looking for candidates? Even a brief moment's thought will show you that we have to insist that Freemasonry is above all a system of morality based on brotherly love, relief and truth and open only to candidates who genuinely believe in God as the Divine Author of our being. This places it firmly in a field of moral conduct which accepts certain standards, particularly those of obedience to a Divine Will, of fairness in our dealings with our fellow human beings and of acceptance, as part of the concept of neighbourliness, of duties in our use of the environment; in other words, of love to God and to our neighbours. We may well feel that this includes tolerance and understanding in our dealings with those of other faiths even though we should remember that insofar as this may involve inter-faith problems in regard to prayer and worship, particularly for some divisions of Christians and Muslims, it could cause problems; but here we enter the realm of theology and important though the concept is, this is neither the time nor the place to try to argue it out and those of us who firmly hold a belief that a solution will be found can only hope and pray that it may come about before religious conflict and the bigotry it begets tears the world apart again.

In this spirit of realism, we have to consider what kind of men come into Freemasonry and why they do or do not enjoy it, since they are, so to speak, the raw material with the development of which we are concerned. We expect Freemasons to have a regard for moral standards; but many men have such a regard and we still have to ask – why do they remain Freemasons? Perhaps we should also ask why some of them resign or cease to attend?

There will be a variety of answers, but it seems fair to suggest that among those who join us there are two main divisions, namely those who are content simply to enjoy the friendship and fellowship of the Craft and those who also feel that Freemasonry stands for ideals they support and in furthering which they believe it is useful that men of good will should band together. There is an important difference between the two groups, since the one will be satisfied with average meetings and convivial refreshment while anyone in the other will gradually withdraw if he feels that we preach but do not practise.

There are however, two elements common to both these views, the first being that of enjoyment. This seems to be the strand which keeps us together; in fact it is enjoyment that makes for a happy gathering, whether in Lodge or Chapter. It is also true that cheerful work and good company create an atmosphere in which ideas develop and constructive plans emerge. There are spin-offs too; wives are more likely to feel that absence on masonic business is not such a bad thing if it brings husbands home contented; candidates are attracted to what is clearly a happy gathering; brethren who are feeling that the world lies heavily on their shoulders are cheered and strengthened; and a little bit more of goodwill is brought into a world that certainly needs it.

Then there is the second element; experience suggests that, so long as we insist that every candidate must in Open Lodge, before everyone present, profess his belief in God and his acceptance of the tenets implicit in the questions asked by the Worshipful Master at the start of the Initiation ceremony, those who originally place their prime emphasis on friendship soon become active supporters of our ideals. We should lose much if we interfered materially with this part of the initiation ceremony, the impact of which is generally unrealised or under-rated.

So far, so good; but that is not enough. Freemasonry, though it is neglected by sociologists almost as much as masonic historians neglect sociology, is a social phenomenon. We may enjoy it but if it is to survive then like all other social phenomena it must either demonstrate that it is relevant to everyday life and so of use to the community in which we live, or decay and vanish under the destroying hand of time. The inevitability of this may not be obvious to those who are strangers to this territory so perhaps some further elaboration is needed.

Your own experience will confirm that social habits change; not many years ago what is now seen as a normal relationship was regarded as "living in sin", women's place was in the home, a child born out of wedlock was stigmatised as a bastard – a word now used to describe the authors of ill-treatment or cruelty or one's cabinet colleagues. Even further back, the rich man lived in his castle and the poor man at his gate by divine dispensation, foreigners were inferior, particularly if they were coloured, and a whole realm of patronising terms were used to describe countrymen of nations which had had the misfortune to have omitted to be British. We must hope that change, though inevitable, will be for the better but whether today's mores are better or worse than yesterday's is not the point here; what we are illustrating is that times do change and that as we live in an envelope of time people inevitably change too. This is a phenomenon recognised by theologians, sociologists and those of other disciplines concerned with human behaviour, but the changes occur gradually and there will often be a considerable lapse of time before they are recognised as such and, when recognised, they will almost certainly be deplored by the elder generation who naturally prefer the customs in which they were brought up. Freemasonry, with its attraction for the elderly, is particularly vulnerable on this score, and the point will become more important and possibly more difficult to deal with in years to come when a much larger proportion of the population is likely to be over 70 years old.

Already the average age of members of a Lodge will in most cases be relatively high and these trends will raise it further still. Freemasonry is already seen by too many as a mere pastime for the middle-aged and elderly and this perception lessens our power to do good in the world. Unless we address the problem the gap between the active young and their still active elders will tend to grow and inevitably, as the "oldies" will neither give up nor adapt, young men will cease to be attracted to Freemasonry. Even if the result is not the decline, decay and death of the Craft it will mean that its impact on the thought and morality of the future will be gravely lessened. No one who thinks about the matter seriously can deny that even now we do not attract as many young men as a society with our ideals should; as long ago as 1979 RW Bro Baillieu, later a much-loved and respected Deputy Grand Master in the English Constitution, pointed to this in a speech in Australia and he went on to touch on something which surely must be of prime importance to the future of the Craft – for remember that without the Craft there will be no Royal Arch. What Bro Baillieu said was, and this is a direct quotation "I am convinced that Masonry requires from us a positive and not a passive role. To be worthy of our principles we must do something in the short span allowed to us to improve the society in which we live; we cannot sit back and leave the task to others." Unfortunately we are far too prone to do just that – leave it to someone else to worry about because "it'll be all right, you'll see". But one day it won't.

This brings us to a most important point, namely that adapting to change should be a positive act; we must not make the mistake of simply drifting with the times. If we are considering the future of a moral movement – and of course Freemasonry with its "system of morality" is such a movement – then we must decide what are the standards which we must maintain. Otherwise we shall not know when to adapt and when to stand fast.

It is fair to suggest that there are two points on which we cannot compromise, first, our insistence that to be a Freemason a man must have a belief in a Divine Creator, and second, that brotherly love, relief and truth, properly understood, are the basis of the system of morality which we profess. These are surely the standards by which as Freemasons we should judge whether or not we can accept any particular change; each of us will also be guided by the tenets of his religion, so there is as it were a double sieve. Remember too that "relief" includes that tolerance of the beliefs of others to which we have already referred. We must not fall into the trap of despising those with other creeds than our own; "judge not that ye be not judged" is a commandment for all time and all people; it well expresses that spirit of tolerance. Equally we must be firm in our individual religious beliefs.

Another point to be considered here is whether we do enough to explain ourselves to those outside the Craft. Privacy may achieve limited objectives but in excess it can self-evidently be defeatist for a movement that aims to impel its members to spread a code of conduct for the governance of social behaviour. The ritual itself tells us that anyone, anyone at all, should know that in distress he or she may prefer a suit to one known to be a Freemason, confident that in doing so the problem is being entrusted to the hands of a person who will act so far as he can, guided not by prejudice but by justice, and who, like the Good Samaritan, will not stop to enquire into personal beliefs or background before trying to help. `How can that happen unless we are prepared to be open about our tenets and about our membership of the Craft as often as that can be done without detriment to ourselves or our connections?

You may wonder whether this is leading us away from the question of the future of the Royal Arch. It certainly is not, but it is reasonable to ask where it is all leading? We have already envisaged the probability that sociological pressures will eliminate or render irrelevant and thus ineffective any social movement that does not meet the perceived needs of the particular time. Freemasonry cannot expect to be an exception to that. Our dated ritual, our code of conduct which can already be considered as being that of yesterday, our hierarchical structure which at first glance is not in sympathy with democratic principles, the closed doors of our lodge rooms which inspire suspicion in the minds of autocratic rulers and other intolerant people in both the religious and political spheres, the generally perceived air of being yesterday's men striving to achieve a come-back: that is how Freemasons may very well come to be regarded if we drift into the next century without thought; and if we are indeed so regarded that will ultimately be the end of the Craft and so of the Royal Arch. It is no answer to maintain that such perceptions distort the truth. We must ask ourselves, as calmly and dispassionately as we can whether Freemasonry should indeed survive? Is it going to be relevant in the next century? It can be; we can be sure of that, but can we feel equally sure that Freemasons will be sufficiently flexible on the one hand and firm enough on the other to recognise, consider and where necessary adapt to changes in society's needs in the rapidly oncoming century?

So what can be done? Of necessity, the views which are now to be put forward will be personal but do please consider them critically. A time is coming, if indeed it is not already here, when many people will feel rootless and insecure, lacking the certainties of an ordered religious belief or even an ordered philosophy for life, their brains mechanised into a computer-based hypnosis, having everything yet conscious of a void in their lives, reaching out as mankind always has done in a yearning for certainty but seeing only an ever-expanding, uncaring, materialist future in a depersonalised universe, the young fighting to establish themselves in control and the old struggling to preserve the illusion of importance, filling out the time while they wait for death. An unnecessarily grim picture? Perhaps. But it is as certain as can be that friendship, companionship and a sense of purpose within a caring and thinking community will be something for which many will long. It may be that things will change and that there will be a reaction and what we might perhaps call scriptural values will return; to meet such a case, it will be even more important that in any reshaping of Freemasonry we should have retained the essential tenets of our profession. In fact, if the Craft can remain in contact with the changes in society and still be true to its fundamental principles, it can indeed have a useful future in such a world; but to remain in contact it will have to rethink its approach. To be useful it must meet needs – the needs of its own members and the needs of others to whom it can bring hope and a sense of purpose.

Take the needs of our own members first. The most important factor will surely be to fire the imagination of each Brother with a sense of the importance and relevance of the Craft. The ritual is dated, but properly approached there can be advantage in that. We can explain to any candidate that we have a ritual which is a literary treasure and which has brought a message to each of us as it did in the days when men had to leave their swords outside the Lodge, when a journey of 50 miles was undertaken with more thought and anxiety than a journey of 5,000 miles commands today, when only the rich could afford the luxury of light and Freemasons tended to govern their meetings by dates when the moon would provide enough for them to see their ways home; we can explain that we treasure that ritual as an heirloom and that it still has its message for us today. A man of the sort we would wish to attract will surely see the force of that and it may help to prepare him for the traditionalist attitude of so many Freemasons which is at once a strength and a weakness.

Then we need to train our members, to explain our organisation and what it can achieve, to absorb them into our friendship in Lodge and at refreshment, and to make clear to them by precept, by example and by teaching, the philosophy on which Freemasonry is based. We must look after our candidates a great deal better than we do now, when they are frequently deserted and left to find their own way once they have been Raised – and also, sad to say, after they have been through the ceremony of Exaltation. This all means that we must devise ways of interesting all our members, new and old, in learning more about their Craft, and train candidates to become teachers in their turn. In former days these functions were performed by the Lectures, but if their wordy and often dated periods have dulled their message for us today because for many years the function of revising them has not been carried out, men of the next century are likely to find them even less acceptable and coherent than we do. New formats are needed which will involve junior and senior members alike and insofar as the work is not undertaken by constitutional authority (of which there is no sign at present) their formation will certainly occasion a considerable amount of work for senior brethren who may have come to think that they have passed the age when "a daily advancement in masonic knowledge" should be sought. Sets of questions and answers each of which would occupy a quarter of an hour might be one possibility; why not write a set for your own Lodge or Chapter now? Ordered expositions of the ceremonies with more detailed suggestions of the lessons they entail and the symbolism they outline are another possibility which the author is grateful to his son for pointing out to him. All this could provide activity for groups of the "oldies" which would be of value to younger members while, in the vernacular, keeping them out of each others' hair and training new generations to take over in their turn. But here a word of warning is appropriate; if you do try your hand at such projects in a Province, you would do well to check your work with the provincial office before you put it into practice.

All this is as relevant to the future of the Royal Arch as to that of the Craft, as you will appreciate. In fact, much of it is, if anything, more important for the Chapter than for the Lodge because in attracting men to the Royal Arch and holding and developing their interest in it we are not only dealing with experienced Freemasons and asking them to give us more of their time but are dealing with a much higher, indeed more profound, level of thought. And dare we suggest that there are too many aspects of the Chapter rituals which still require attention insofar as they are irrelevant, outdated and unhelpful? There's heresy for you! But if you doubt it, consider the lectures and even the passages of scripture in the ritual, not least in the Installation ceremonial. Then here is another thought which has already been mentioned in passing: should we give up the Royal Arch as a separate order and treat it as a fourth Craft degree? This would not be as heretical as it may sound, nor would it interfere with "ancient landmarks", for it would only be reverting to the practice of the Grand Lodge of the "Antients" before the Union of 1813; it could be an enormous boost for the Royal Arch, which has never recovered from relative neglect at that time and the separation then forced upon it under the pretence of union.

Before you start to throw brickbats or any heavy item of lodge furniture that may be to hand by way of protest, let us turn hastily to the needs of those not of our fraternity; here too we need a radical rethink. Our attitude to them constitutes our shop-window and it must be attractively decked out with taste, modesty and decorum. We are too prone to find a cause, support it for a while and then, as other Masters come along with other ideas, to feel that we have done the job and can forget it. There are two things particularly which it may be suggested should be done as a matter of course. The first is that when we step in to help we should decide, and make clear to all concerned, the precise extent of our help, and then, when that has been achieved, explain that if further help is needed later, it should be asked for then and the request will be reconsidered in the light of circumstances then prevailing: in other words, the initiative should be left with the recipient. In that way misunderstanding and disappointment which might otherwise sour the reputation of Freemasonry will be avoided. The second thing is that in preference to the newspaper type of publicity we should simply leave something on site as it were – a placard, for instance, or photograph, even a representation of a square and compasses, visibly indicating that we have helped, publicity at the point of sale, so to speak; if a general device were agreed it could become recognised by the general public as our signature. Other kinds of publicity may be very well at times but they are not always welcomed by the recipient and can eventually give the impression that the work is done for the sake of the publicity and not simply because it is what we do. We might even think of the possibility of some badge such as the wearing of an ostensibly masonic tie when a Brother is on such an errand of mercy.

Now let us get back to the main thread and think about how the ideas put forward in this paper might have particular application to the Royal Arch. Whatever its supporters may say, there are too many Companions who are either ambivalent about it or simply find it boring. We have to accept this as a fact but we do not do enough to consider whether at least some of the criticism may be justified; if we conclude that it may be, then it is urgent that we should do something to put matters right for inaction could spell disaster for the Order. To take this on board we must be clear on the role of the Chapter in Freemasonry and if necessary reconsider aspects of the ritual; for the present it may be enough to say that it is the completion of the Third Degree, but its full role is something to which we must return later. Next, we need to project a definite image to the Lodges, something which would be much easier to do if we did in fact bring the Royal Arch under the Lodge warrant. Clearly wearing the Royal Arch jewel on all Craft occasions is important but there are also many opportunities for stressing that being a Companion of the Order means accepting the highest standards of Brotherly Love, Relief and Truth and expanding one's thoughts into the realm of the eternal; and we should emphasise by example that the Royal Arch, like the Craft, is to be enjoyed. Remember what was said a few moments ago about the role of Freemasonry in the next century; we must get the message across that the needs of the time are met in an even deeper sense in the Royal Arch. It is not the pretence of superior knowledge that will attract Brethren and there is an element of naivety in thinking that it will. Pressure to join is unlikely to produce a satisfactory candidate. Brethren should see that members of the Chapter are enthusiasts, practical yet idealists, thoughtful about our life and its purpose, and that they enjoy the companionship of the Royal Arch; candidates should be attracted, not dragooned. It should be made clear that it takes time to understand the full message of the Order, so that there will be no disappointment when a new companion realises that progression may be slow and that there is only the one ceremony, apart from Installation. Above all, you should so conduct yourself in Lodge that it will be obvious that Companions of the Royal Arch are among the most friendly and helpful members of the Lodge and have a particular interest in the welfare and progress of newcomers into Freemasonry and that means they must never be regarded simply as potential cannon-fodder.

The author of the paper now has to risk being accused of conceit because in returning to consider something which was deferred earlier, the full role of the Chapter, he intends to try to do this by reference to what he has already written in two places. The first is in the booklet *Why Join the Royal Arch?* which is intended as something which can be given to a Master Mason but which hopefully all of you have read. It is in fact an abbreviation of a talk he had the privilege of giving to the Supreme Grand Chapter of Italy in happier days, a task the prospect of which called for much thought about the subject. What is said in it, that for a Freemason the Royal Arch completes the meaning of the third of our three principles, Truth, seems to have met with general approval and a reference to it here may be excused by the fact that the profits from its sale go to Quatuor Coronati Correspondence Circle Ltd whose surplus funds are devoted not to its members but to the furtherance of masonic education and charity.

The second reference comes from *Understanding the Royal Arch* the author's royalties from which come to a Provincial Benevolent Fund, and as this extract so fully represents his view he places it before you as a conclusion to this talk without further comment other than to say that there is no reason why you should not quote it to a prospective candidate if you wish. So here is the quotation:

> "The Royal Arch teaches us that as the grandeur, the perils and the struggles of this world, which seem so important now, grow meaningless with time and pass as the glory of Solomon's temple and the captivity of his people both passed, so too do the disappointment and frustration fade as we realize that there is a meaning to life because we are the creatures of a Creator Who has his purpose for each of us and Whom it is our bounden duty to revere in accordance with the teachings of religion, however we may worship and whatever the individual's religious belief. In the final analysis the legend of the Craft is one of failure and loss, a story of the victory of mortality. The Royal Arch transforms that legend and its teaching by placing them in a framework of eternity and so gives them perspective and meaning within the context of religion. That is the great lesson and the reason why it is the completion of our system."

And that, let us add, is why it should last as long as the system itself lasts.

[The original of this talk ended up by asking "So now, has anyone got some matches, a length of rope and a stake?" but it seems unfair that anyone reading it in Chapter should be asked to endanger himself in that way, so the final sentence has been omitted from the text!]

PART FOUR
LOOKING TO THE FUTURE

13
Can Freemasonry Survive

The two final papers of this collection look to Freemasonry's future and the challenges and opportunities that it may face in the 21st century. This paper deals with how changing attitudes may affect the public's perception of the Craft and how the Craft might react to it. Is it in fact adequately poised to thrive in the world of the future? The following paper is concerned more particularly with internal matters such as whether alterations or adaptations are needed in our own procedures to ensure that they remain relevant and to establish what are the constraints to be observed if any action is to be taken. The objective in each case is to start discussion about this and the author has not hesitated to make radical suggestions with which not everyone will agree; but discussion is needed and it will not be fruitful unless even the unthinkable is thought about.

It is interesting to note once again the parallels that exist in this matter of adapting to changing times for all sciences concerned with human behaviour. For instance, the following extract from a publication of the Doctrine Commission of the Church of England applies to Freemasonry just as to the Church of England:

> *"The wise man apportions his belief to the evidence" wrote David Hume. Free enquiry must take place, and if it does not lead to orthodoxy, then this is part of the liberty that must be granted to the human mind.*

Freemasonry has no inbuilt immortality. Those of us who earnestly believe in its value in the life of our community, our country and the world have to think, and think hard about its future and even about the possibility of the demise of the Craft. That may sound extreme but a few moments' thought should convince you of the possibilities and of the problems of survival, in the world of the 21st century into which we are moving, for a movement founded in the form in which we know it in the early 18th century, well before the Industrial Revolution. And remember, serious thinking carries no government health warning and may indeed be good for us.

Freemasonry is in a way involved with theology, in that a belief in a Supreme Being is the cardinal requirement for membership; that requirement we must retain. Basically the Craft is a social phenomenon and as that point is essential to the arguments advanced in this paper we should spend some time considering whether it is a correct statement, because if it is then the Craft as we know it must inevitably change or perish or decay into one of those survivals which are the fond darlings of eccentric and usually rather sentimental and doddering old dears whose only contribution to society has become the amusement they give to those few on whom their activities (such as they may be) impinge, or to whose notice they are drawn by a cynical press. So what proof is there? A large number of authorities for the proposition could be quoted from philosophy, sociology or any other science dealing with the business of living, but one should be sufficient and it is in fact taken from a work on theology discussing a similar problem in the sphere of religion – "We depend upon developed traditions which nevertheless, if they are to remain alive, requires that we respond to them openly, critically and creatively." That statement is particularly useful because it accepts the need for change but points out with great clarity the parameters which must be observed: namely, response to a tradition which has stood the test of time, but which must always be subject to open but constructive critical examination.

Clearly we cannot embark on such a survey unless we know what it is that we are surveying; so we must start by defining Freemasonry as it is practised here today. There are many definitions but there seems to be general agreement that the best is one which is indeed enshrined in something about which we must think in the course of our investigations, our rituals. That definition is of course "a peculiar system of morality, veiled in allegory and illustrated by symbols", though even those familiar words contain a trap into which we may very easily fall, the way in which words can change their generally accepted meaning. In the days when the ritual we use was being formulated "peculiar" did not have the implication of oddity or strangeness which it has today; it denoted uniqueness and even carried the stamp of admiration. It does not necessarily follow that we should therefore change the ritual in this respect but it does point out once more that we cannot isolate ourselves from changes in the world around us. If the very words which we use to define what we are doing have changed their meaning we may end up by giving a totally wrong impression about our objectives to an outside enquirer.

Another keyword in the definition is "system". It is generally accepted that the basis of the "system" is the old trilogy: "brotherly love, relief and truth", the two last including not only charity (another word which has changed its primary meaning) but also toleration of the beliefs of others. For our immediate purposes, and with a full appreciation of the original meaning of these words, we can accept the definition. It is a matter of importance because it establishes the parameters for what we should regard as fundamental to our appreciation of the problem and which will provide the basis from which we must work, since without any one of them we should no longer be talking about Freemasonry as we know it. We might even do well to recognise them as ancient landmarks.

If you accept what has been put forward so far then you must surely agree that such teaching places Freemasonry squarely in the context of social behaviour and as it is a voluntary movement in the sense that there is no compulsion to join, there will be no wish to join unless it is seen to be relevant or advantageous; as we try to exclude those who would join for "mercenary or other unworthy motive" we are left with the proposition that at any particular time our system must be seen as relevant to the society in which we live. That means that Freemasonry must change with changing times, and in case you still doubt that let me bring two statements to your notice by way of support, one by a professor of philosophy and the other by a theologian. Martin Hollis, professor of philosophy at the University of East Anglia has written "The modern map of heaven and earth took the shape, which we now broadly accept, only in the 16th and 17th centuries"; and here is a quotation from David Brown who is a university lecturer in theology at Oxford: "because historical circumstances change, it is only by a religion being ready to alter its expression and emphasis that it can hope to preserve its essential content and message". In the same way, every masonic researcher knows that we cannot hope to follow the arguments of even the masonic writers of the first half of the 18th century unless we know something of pre-Darwinian beliefs.

It has been worth spending some time on this because most Freemasons, with their strong sense of tradition, have an inbuilt bias against change. What has been said so far in this paper shows that in a rapidly changing world we cannot take it for granted that all Freemasonry has to do to survive is nothing, because what is relevant today may not apply in the world into which we are advancing. It follows that we must try to look at how our world may change but we can only do this to a very limited extent. However, trends are developing today which may give some shape to tomorrow and we can say at once that deterioration in moral standards must concern any movement which upholds the highest standards, particularly one which relies on voluntary recruitment for its continued existence.

All this of course must be seen in context. If Freemasonry abandoned belief in its system of morality it would no longer be Freemasonry. What we are, or should be concerned about is presentation, the public image we must project if we are to attract the type of recruit we need to keep the flame burning brightly. We even have to ask ourselves if there is any reason why Freemasonry should survive; what does it contribute to society? Is it too inward looking? Is it elitist? Is the ritual out-of-date and if so, does it matter? It does not follow that just because we enjoy our Freemasonry now a future generation will do so. We should ask ourselves what the needs of our successors will be and what will be their social mores. So unless we think we are just in the Craft to enjoy ourselves – something we certainly hope to do, but hardly the be-all-and-end-all for a system of morality – there are two things to think about here: first, what are we trying to do that is worthwhile and of public benefit; and second, what modifications to the way in which we present ourselves and our message – for it is a message for others as much as for ourselves – are called for? As an example of this latter point think about whether the man of the next century will wish to attend meetings at night, particularly in large cities, with all the problems of night-time travel? Will his wife feel he should not go out socially without her? Will television or its successor have taken such hold on our lives that we will sit all evening with eyes fixed squarely – no pun intended – squarely on the "box"? Will cyberspace and virtual reality have effectively displaced social activity or will they produce a reaction which favours it?

As to what we are trying to achieve, that surely is implicit in the definition of Freemasonry we have accepted. We take our stand on a belief in a Divine Creator and acceptance of standards of morality which can effectively be summed up in duty to God and to our neighbours – surely worthy aims of benefit to our community. It is of course fashionable today to lament and even despair of the moral state of society. But this is nothing new; it is a recurring phenomenon – people rebel against a strict moral code and then swing against the relaxation that ensues; it is a never ending cycle and we would be wrong if we allowed our teaching to swing with it. But our method of teaching may well have to alter as the years go by if men are to continue to be attracted to join us. Therein lies the possibility of paradox, for if we stray from our basic tenets we can no longer consider ourselves to be Freemasons, but if we are thought to be irrelevant and to be struggling to preserve an outdated world we shall not attract the kind of men who will keep the torch alight when we have gone. We have to realise too how very limited our appeal seems to be; are we too complaisant about this? Why are there so few Freemasons on the shop-floor? Or round the board-room table? Or in the world of the trade unions? How does what we contribute to charity compare with what we spend on refreshment after lodge? What work do we do for charity? Do we contribute enough to local causes?

Where does all this lead us? Surely to the suggestion that we must be more open about ourselves if the Craft is to be seen to be relevant to the society in which it exists; that in fact is the only way to resolve the paradox. At one time men did join us because of curiosity and a desire to know something allegedly secret. No longer. So much has been stripped away and so much exposed that it is doubtful whether any such motivation exists now; nor should we lament the fact. Unless as Freemasons we are known to adopt and try to live by the highest moral standards, men whose help as members of the Craft is worth having will not be attracted to join it. Publicity will not do it but example and a willingness to discuss our Craft and our reasons for enjoying it will. It is because of this belief that a booklet was recently published which some have criticised as too revealing, though most who have seen it seem to have welcomed it: *Notes for a Candidate for Freemasonry*. Lodge meetings should be known as happy occasions on which likeminded men can provide each other with support for upholding the high standards they have set themselves.

All this is a matter of personal behaviour but there should surely be no objection to stating publicly, for instance that you could or could not approve a particular course because of the masonic principles you have promised to observe, and in such a case it would clearly be right to explain what the principle was which you felt would be infringed; there is nothing sanctimonious in standing up for worthy principles and while we should do this so far as possible "without detriment to ourselves or connections" we do have to face the question of what support we do or should give to those who do so, perhaps to their own detriment – but that is not something we can deal with here.

The question of public attitudes and duties is one side of the matter, but we still have to consider whether and to what extent we should alter our behaviour in lodge. Here is contentious ground. One Scottish clan has a slogan "Touch not the cat bote (for the benefit of Sassenachs that means 'without') – bote a glove". A similar caution applies to masonic ritual. We are all well aware of the danger here but in so important a matter as the future of the Craft there can be no questions that must not be asked. We should regard our ritual as a treasure from the past and explain it as such to candidates, urging them to concentrate on the lessons it contains and to admire the language of the silver age of English literature of which it is in general so excellent an example, though there is certainly at least one later addition which it would be joy to see expunged – one which applies Archbishop Ussher's biblical chronology to the date of creation of the world.

Again, the average mason should be helped to become acquainted with the historic background of the Order. Even a rudimentary knowledge of our past can be of great help in dealing with the anxieties of genuine enquirers and the often unrecognised wish of brethren, particularly newcomers, to know more about the why and the wherefore. And while on that point let us consider something of great importance to the future of our lodges but which we so often neglect: the instruction of candidates. Do you remember how you felt at your second lodge meeting? Having been the star of the first you were now slung out of the lodge room and left to your own devices, sometimes not even allowed to see the preparation of the candidate for the ceremony. There is too often a tendency to regard the "new boy" as a kindergarten entry. We, and especially those of us who feel conscious of our seniority, must remember at all times that we are not dealing with immature kids but with grown men who in many cases will have proved their value to the community and be held in respect, or even awe, by others. Surely we should at least see that a candidate is looked after on such occasions. A senior brother or perhaps a steward should welcome the opportunity to retire with the candidate and tell him something about the Craft of which he is a member and of the lodge which he has joined. But if that is done, there must be careful consideration of how the time will be spent so as to benefit the new member, and that will entail preparation and careful planning and should not be an occasion for showing off one's own knowledge.

That may have been a diversion, but it is an important, indeed vital, matter for the future and so can justifiably claim a place in our thoughts at this point. Now we come back to the main thrust of our quest and put two questions, for you to think about. No answers will be suggested, each of us has to work through such problems for himself, though this will be helped by discussion. The questions are very simple: the first is "why": why should Freemasonry survive? In other words, what has it done and what can it do to deserve to survive? Some thoughts about this have already been suggested, but do they provide an adequate answer? The second is "What must we do to ensure that Freemasonry meets the needs of the next century?" In answering this it may be helpful to consider the relevance of three points in particular: first, as has already been questioned, whether it is true that there are two important classes of men whom we do not seem to attract, at least not to a degree which would reflect their importance in the community, the business executive and the shop-floor workman; second, while we would wish to preserve our integrity, whether we can expect to attract men if we will not talk about ourselves and acknowledge our membership of the Craft and be clear about the reasons for maintaining and enjoying that membership; and third, whether it is at least arguable that we do not do enough to draw non-masons, including the ladies, into our activities, for instance by combining in charitable initiatives and letting it be known that we do so as part of our duty as Freemasons.

Whatever answers we give to these points we still must face the fact that if we hide our light under a bushel we are not going to be noticed. From a recruiting point of view we have first to gain attention and here there is nothing to equal the facts that you obviously enjoy your Freemasonry, and that you are prepared to talk about it; if it were a social club or something of that sort to which you enjoyed going, you would want to share your enjoyment with your friends. Unless there is a specific problem, as for instance prejudice against the Craft by an employer, it seems nonsense to have inhibitions about letting people know that you are a Freemason and that you enjoy your Freemasonry, particularly if you believe that the Craft makes a worthwhile contribution towards preserving social standards of morality. These inhibitions of the past are allowed to repress us far too much but their legacy is the misunderstanding and acrimony which we still have to endure and which can make men wary of admitting their membership. Caution is a good thing so far as it inhibits bringing men in who do not accept the responsibility of living by our standards but subject to that we must do what we can to displace by our actions the misplaced hostility which our past withdrawal has encouraged. It will not always be easy to do so.

Now, what about the pattern of our meetings? They still bear the stamp of the 18th century: a business meeting followed by a banquet, now downgraded to dinner or supper. There is a strong case for occasional meetings with no ceremony and surely there is no reason why we should feel inhibited on such occasions from entertaining non-masons. The pattern would be to open, call off, receive the guest or guests, have a talk or discussion after which the non-masons would be escorted to the bar while the lodge was called on and closed, everyone then dining together or having a buffet meal. The non-masonic guest might be from the local clergy, civic life, some charity, perhaps a worker from a third world country – anyone who had something interesting and relevant to say or who wanted to ask us questions. Clearly it would be essential in a Province to clear the matter with the Provincial Grand Master, or in London with the Grand Secretary's office. Being allowed to come into the lodge room and see the brethren sitting there in regalia can be an attraction and bridges can be built and fences mended in the atmosphere of the after-proceedings. Such meetings could do much to promote understanding and to keep Freemasonry socially relevant. Perhaps you might even be allowed to entertain lady masons in this way one day.

Finally, be daring in your thinking but cautious in your action. It is true to say that over the last two centuries Freemasonry has slowly changed, but too often the need for change has not been foreseen; and imploring the aid of the landmarks can be an excuse for refusal to think. Change in any social movement is essential if it is to survive but no such change should ever prejudice the main purpose of the movement any more than it should be undertaken on grounds of temporary expediency; better that the movement should cease to exist. Some will nevertheless criticise you for daring to question their version of the landmarks; but you should rightly be unrepentant so long as the principles to which we have already referred are not prejudiced but are carefully preserved wherever the future may lead. That, after all, is what is really important.

14
Which may seriously damage your complacency

Why should Freemasonry survive in the 21st century? After all, it is not a necessity, like food and drink. True, it has survived more or less in the form in which we know it for at least two centuries in which the world has changed out of all recognition; it may help us with the answer if we try to understand why it has done so. Then, if we can decide what may lie ahead for our descendants in the 21st century we can try to see whether it is likely that Freemasonry as we know it will appeal to them as relevant, helpful and enjoyable; for we must keep in mind the important fact that activities which are seen as out-of-date or inappropriate to the social order of the times decay and die. How is it then that for nearly three centuries Freemasonry has been seen as relevant to a society which has changed beyond what could have been imagined to our predecessors in 1717?

In looking back over the years it is often assumed that the Craft as we know it has not changed materially since those early days. The assumption is false. Even in modern times there have been changes. There is a greater emphasis on openness than there was half a century ago, but a century before that public masonic processions, particularly those to parish churches before such meetings as that of Provincial Grand Lodge, and ceremonies such as the laying of foundation stones were a well known feature of public life. The penalties in the obligations have disappeared, so has one of the recognition words in the Royal Arch. Even the ritual, for all that it is so revered, has been revised drastically; at the time of the Union of the two rival English Grand Lodges in 1813 the Duke of Sussex as Grand Master ensured that was so. It is worth noting too that there were Anglican priests on the committee which presided over the revision, even though one of its tasks was to ensure the removal of christian references from it. One of them, Bro Hemmant was particularly active in this, as we know from the biting comments of Bro Rev Dr Oliver, then known in many countries as the sage and historian of the Craft, and in whose opinion Freemasonry was and would remain a christian movement.

If we think about this matter of change, then, we shall realise that it has happened in the past and that it is in fact inevitable. Freemasonry is a social phenomenon and as such it is part of everyday life; to survive it must therefore be relevant to that life and be seen as relevant. This will only come about if its basic tenets are seen as relevant, and if its methods and procedures in furthering those tenets appeal to the men it should attract in the society of the day as contributing to their enjoyment and supporting and strengthening their moral and religious conceptions. Each of us can see from his own knowledge how much society has changed and is changing. For one instance take the case of the computer; much work which was done not many years ago on a typewriter is today done with a computer and word-proccessing software, terms that would be understood by very few people even 20 years ago. On a grander scale, our conceptions about the physical nature of the universe have changed with the acceptance of quantum mechanics and the uncertainty principle, so much so that in some quarters these have been seen as casting doubt on long-cherished religious views; the sanctity of the Bible itself has been questioned by such authors as Robin Lane Fox; theologians have had to reconsider long-held positions while still maintaining fundamental religious beliefs. In other disciplines too change has been on a startling scale. We can now examine building plans in three dimensions and wander round buildings which have not yet been constructed; and we can put ourselves into the non-world of cyberspace. All these developments have taken place within a lifetime, and the momentum continues. When such vast changes occur our conception of what is true and what is relevant is affected and social history records another advance – or as some might think, another retreat. We have to ask ourselves whether Freemasonry can remain relevant in such a world; will it too have to change in order to survive? Can it change? Will future initiations take place in a virtual reality construction of King Solomon's temple with the brethren in their separate homes, linked together by the internet? These are extreme suggestions, but the mere fact that they can be recognised as possible means that we have to consider what we do and why we do it.

Freemasons are chary of change. Their insistence on the sanctity of landmarks is a proof of that. That may be a virtue but it can be a hindrance; we do have to be careful about it but we must not ignore the necessity. Freemasonry has survived changes in the past, but they were always changes of method, not substance, changes within a context , the context of its basic tenets. Change in basic tenets is something we should certainly rule out as impossible; it would rightly be thought of as removal of landmarks. Change in method however, is another matter; if it is inevitable it can be effected without damage to the fabric of the Order provided that what is needed is appreciated in time. In the past alterations in social patterns and mores have come about gradually and in general there has been ample time in which to appreciate their effect and to adapt. But today events and inventions are occurring so rapidly that it is difficult to keep pace with the advancement of the frontiers of knowledge and the alterations in our way of living that they produce. The advent of television was gradual compared with the impact of computer-based activities.

Freemasonry is, as has so often been stressed in these papers, a social phenomenon and in that sense it has similarities to religion in the realm of social science. It is therefore apposite to quote a typical passage from the writings of a modern theologian on this problem of change; he wrote:

> "... arguably one of the major sources of the continuing strength of religion is its realisation that one must change in order to remain the same. That is to say, because historical circumstances change, it is only by a religion being ready to alter its expression and emphasis that it can hope to preserve its essential content and message." [David Brown: *Invitation to Theology* 1989. See too *We Believe in God* by the Doctrine Commission of the Church of England, 1987.]

Similar considerations apply to other social phenomena such as Freemasonry; once any such movement becomes thought of as irrelevant, it may continue for a while as a hobby for the curious or even suffer the ultimate indignity of being relegated to the status of an object the only interest of which is as the subject of historical research; but it will no longer attract followers interested in fostering it; and where, as with Freemasonry, we are talking about something undertaken voluntarily, failure to attract new followers means an inevitable decline into oblivion.

This kind of argument will no doubt come as a culture shock to some. But it is a fact of life, proved again and again down the ages, that what is perceived as losing its relevance falls into limbo; we must remember that the future is already in the womb of the present.

Consider some examples of this process of obsolescence. The stage-coach would be one, the tea clipper boat another; both were overtaken by other, speedier, more reliable modes of travel. So it has been with mental processes and skills; the typewriter has lost its primacy in mechanical production of written communication; the word-processor is more convenient because it allows the material to be previewed and corrections to be made easily. Quantum mechanics and the uncertainty principle have in turn modified the work of Newton and Einstein. Change is as endemic in today's world as it always has been; the difference between yesterday and today is that now it happens more often and more quickly – running faster to remain in the same place like a demented Red Queen.

Now look again at the theological quotation already noted. It implies that "the essential content and message" remain. The whole reason for the changes is to remain the same, that is, to present what is essential in a manner which will make it understandable, relevant and satisfying for the present. So we have to decide what is essential, what must be preserved, before we can determine what, if anything, might with advantage be changed. This is why it is so important to understand what Freemasonry essentially is and one factor in assessing that will be an examination of the past and an assessment of the reasons why the Craft has outlasted great changes in the past; for it has survived them and proportionately they may be compared to what is happening today and will happen tomorrow. What then is the basis of what we are anxious to preserve? What is the essence of Freemasonry? We are not concerned here with Freemasonry outside the lodge room; that is an important subject in its own right in this context. What matters for us here is what is done in lodge, which is where the lessons are taught and learned.

One answer to the question of what we must take care to preserve has so consistently been given that we can regard it as accepted: "a system of morality, veiled in allegory and illustrated by symbols [based on] brotherly love, relief and truth". That definition gives us two important clues. First, allegory and symbolism are important as methods of communication; and second, there are verities on which the system is based, the triad of love, relief and truth which can be summarised as love to God and love to one's neighbour or even more briefly as caring. In the kind of world into which we seem to be advancing so quickly the one worldly reality will still be that we have to deal with our fellows; and the one great mystery will still be that of the Creation and the Creator. There will be some who will reject or fly from considering the latter but the history of humanity in all ages and all climes shows that anxiety and curiosity about these two relationships is deeply woven into human consciousness. They are the basic concerns of religion and though Freemasonry is not a religion Dr Oliver, whose work can be too readily denigrated in the light of further knowledge and better and more available research tools, may have glimpsed a truth when he called the Craft "a handmaid of religion". A Freemason has to have a religion for he cannot be admitted into the Craft without an open profession of his belief in God. The essence of Freemasonry may be defined as honouring that belief and developing the caring qualities for the Creator's world that such a belief requires.

How then do we go about this? The definition refers to allegory and symbolism. Down the ages and in every country and every type of social climate stories have been a means of instruction, of driving lessons home. It is possible to interest people in stories when they will not listen to sermons. The stories may not be true; indeed, the best are probably untrue, about events which never happened or at least not in the form in which the narrator placed them. But they are magic. The New Testament parables are vivid examples of the effectiveness of such teaching. The Hiramic legend is another example. The appeal is to the senses – of wonder, excitement, fear, joy, for example. The hearer remembers them.

So too with symbolism. No Freemason can see a mason's square or level without remembering the moral attributes attributed to them. There is probably no better way than the use of allegory and symbolism to make moral teaching acceptable and memorable. For Freemasons, this is what the ritual is about. The lessons it teaches are timeless and it really does not matter whether we believe in the events as told or not.

We do however, have a problem with the ritual, one already noted in an earlier paper – the changing meaning of words. This is a matter which urgently requires review although such a notion will bring cries of outrage from some earnest and sincere brethren. But where survival is at stake one has to reconsider even fondly cherished shibboleths. Except in the Royal Arch ritual, very little is required and that little would come under the head of minor adjustment.

To emphasise this point consider two examples. In the 18th century the word "speculative" would not have the vaguely derogatory meaning attaching to it today but would unhesitatingly be understood as implying thoughtful consideration. Should we change it? If so, to what? Probably our nearest single word today would be "contemplative"; to change would probably be too great a culture shock, but perhaps a qualifying explanation would be helpful for the "new boy" – for instance, "you will realise that 'speculative' in the phrase 'speculative Freemasonry' refers to our use of allegory and symbolism to teach brethren the system of morality of which you have already heard".

The second example perhaps cheats a little because it comes from the ritual of a degree of the Ancient and Accepted Rite; but it so clearly illustrates the point that hopefully you will not feel it to be inappropriate in a book about the Craft. In the ritual of one degree the candidate is told "The reward of prudence is understanding": does that make sense today? How does being prudent increase your understanding of a problem? You may even feel that being prudent might prevent you from understanding it. But now consider the meaning of the word "prudence" to our ancestors in the 17th and early 18th centuries. The educated man would immediately recognise it as one of the virtues described by Cicero and having three parts: memory, intelligence and foresight. Apply that definition and the sentence makes clear sense: acquired knowledge, appreciation of its relevance, and a reasoned assessment of the future should indeed give rise to understanding.

There are however, certain interpolations which have been inserted into the ritual and are so obviously nonsensical that their continued inclusion is ridiculous. The statement about a certain death occurring at a given period from the Creation is ludicrous in the face of modern knowledge; not only that, it is obvious to every candidate to whom it is seriously communicated that it is nonsense. As a heretic, I either omit it or rephrase it myself and say "after the traditional date for . . ."; but such individual alterations are not a satisfactory solution. The sentence is a late interpolation – an effort by our predecessors to show how up-to-date with the latest knowledge they were, in this case Archbishop Ussher's chronology for biblical events finally published in 1654 and which still appears in the margins of many editions of the Authorised Version of the Bible. The reference should be expunged from our ritual because first, it serves no useful purpose, second, it is based on false theory and third, it is clear to everyone who hears it that it is rubbish.

Another example is the wording which compels us to tell a candidate that he is now permitted to "extend his researches" into the hidden mysteries of nature and science", matters about which a young candidate may well know much more than his elderly instructor.

When we come to the Royal Arch, however, there are more serious problems; some of them have been discussed elsewhere in this collection and need not be repeated here. They arise from two main causes. The first is that the second and third lectures are couched in obfuscating and outdated language as well as being too long; consequently they cannot be conveniently given together at one meeting and are unlikely to retain the attention of the candidate at the end of a long ceremony. The second cause is that the welfare of the Royal Arch and its ritual were neglected at the time of the Union in 1813 and it is still perceived as separate from the Craft although its teaching is essential to complete that of the Craft degrees.

My heretical proposals here would be, first, that the second and third lectures should be rewritten and second, that steps should be taken to integrate the Craft and Chapter and revert to the "Antients' " practice of working the Royal

Arch under the Craft warrant. There would no doubt be outraged cries about the ancient landmarks; but the ritual has not been exempt from change in the past and so by definition it cannot be a landmark. There will also be the assertion that the Grand Lodge does not interfere with ritual; that is nonsense because it has done so, most notably in the Duke of Sussex's time and in the recent matter of the penalties. There may of course be other solutions to the problems. But make no mistake, we shall increasingly be seen as tarred with the brush of absurdity if our ritual, now no longer private, is held up as out-of-touch with reality. We have no reason to be ashamed of its allegorical or mythical content which has served, serves and will continue to serve Freemasons well; we should indeed be proud of it, but there is no excuse for perpetuating irrelevant and uninstructive absurdities. There are very few alterations that are needed to remove these ridiculous anomalies.

One aspect of our teaching tradition which has become neglected is the lectures and it is worth while thinking for a moment about why this is so. It is in part this same question of outdated language but in this case further complications are that the content of the "established" lectures contains moral musings of a length which exceeds the attention span of the average man of today and is perceived as either irrelevant or even in some cases inaccurate. A new method is needed if the function of the lectures in leading brethren to think about our symbolism and allegories and all that is implicit in the system of morality we profess is to be revived. There is much of value in the lectures and it should not be lost. We do not have to follow the question and answer form of the past; it can for instance be done by a review of a ceremony as has been done in one lodge and found to be effective. There will be other methods. But encouragement and experiment are needed. The rewards are great; the enjoyment of an unusual evening and an increase in masonic knowledge are two of the benefits and it is one way of maintaining "the essential content and message" of Freemasonry and so the interest of the brethren.

It will now be as well to allow a period for cooling-off by summarising the lessons which emerge from the past and from our vision of the future. There cannot be a categoric statement about this; each of us will have his own ideas. On the basic point of whether Freemasonry will and should survive, the answer will depend on whether it meets tomorrow's needs. The author's own view has already been given – that there will be a place for the Craft in tomorrow's world because its teaching and its ideal of brotherhood meet basic needs of humanity for which there may be little space in the future, but that its survival will depend on the removal of anomalies and the careful editing of what is now seen as ridiculous or without meaning in the ritual.

We have to face the problem squarely – that is not intended as a pun. Should we shut up the shop, call it a day, retire to lick our wounds, or adopt whatever other such course the similes of past years may suggest? Emphatically not, so long as we have something of value to contribute to society and to the thought of the individuals who make up that society. That we do indeed have such a contribution to make no-one who understands Freemasonry can dispute. Let us think again about the theological quotation we considered earlier. Our care at all times must be to preserve the "essential content and message", and that surely must mean brotherly love, relief and truth taught by allegory and symbol. These are lasting needs for any civilised society and there will always be a place in that society for a movement which teaches them in a form which has been tried and proved down the ages but moulded to suit the new social climate and attention span. It is not helpful in this matter to say that men ought to listen; they will vote with their feet if that attitude is adopted. But they will understand the ritual as a treasure from the past once it is purged of statements which, however rational they were considered to be three (or even two) centuries ago, are now universally recognised as inaccurate, and once words which have changed their meaning are altered or enlarged upon. They will also understand and appreciate the allegory and symbolism; and Freemasonry will continue to serve humanity for many years to come.